NUDGED BY SPIRIT

HOW THE FATHER I NEVER KNEW INFLUENCED ME FROM THE AFTERLIFE AND AWAKENED MY PSYCHIC ABILITIES

DIANE FRANCES

COPPER CANOPY PRESS

Copyright © 2021 by Diane Frances

Copper Canopy Press

All rights reserved.

No part of this book may be reproduced in any form or by any electronic or mechanical means, including information storage and retrieval systems, without written permission from the author, except for the use of brief quotations in a book review.

Cover art by Lauren Mazzola

LaurenMazzola.com

Author Photo by Jo Bryan Photography LLC

To my sister Dawn for encouraging me to tell this story from my perspective and without hesitation. I look forward to the years we have ahead of us.

To my father, with gratitude. I will see you soon enough.

ONE

NUDGED

April 24, 2011

Today is my father's birthday. I never knew him, and he's dead. I've always known his name and I met him once, but that was a disaster. (I'll come back to that later.) I can't explain why I decided to look for him exactly today, because I've thought about searching several times in my life. In the end, I figured if he wanted to know me, he knew where to find me. It's his loss, not mine. But two days ago I felt an overwhelming urge to look.

I started on Facebook with the name my mother had given me, and found several possibilities. I looked at each one, and stopped in my tracks with one photo. This was my half-brother; there was no doubt in my mind. I could see the resemblance to me and my oldest son and I knew in my gut he was my brother. I messaged him but didn't reveal why. "I'm looking for Paul Pantano, who is 70 to 80 years old. He grew up around Brook Avenue in New York City. Do you know him?"

He responded "You may mean my father. He grew up in the Bronx, not sure about Brook Ave. Unfortunately he passed away in 2007. He would have been 76 today. My mom is still around, Carol Schrouder was her maiden name. She lives in Boston with my sister. If you'd like to get in touch with her let me know and I will arrange it for you. Take care." I sat there stunned for a few moments. I couldn't believe it. I had finally decided that I wanted to talk to him and I was too late. I would never be able to ask him why he hadn't called and why he abandoned me.

I responded that I was sorry to hear that, but didn't want to bother his mother. I asked where he was buried, thinking I could go to his grave and have the conversation I needed to have with him. I thought it was odd that he never asked me why I was looking for his father... I finally let the cat out of the bag and told my brother who I was although I'd previously decided not to tell him. After all, I was coming out of the blue after 40+ years. Did I really want to disrupt his reality with my existence? In that moment in the private messenger conversation, something pushed me. It was just like whatever had pushed me to look for my father in the first place.

"He was my father too," I wrote.

He didn't respond for a few moments, but then started firing questions at me. I hesitated to respond. "Oh no, you can't drop a bomb like that and then just disappear" he wrote. "I need to know how you know this, who you are, when you were born? Was it before or after he married my mother? Who's your mother? I don't know what to say... I'm truly shocked if it's true. Where are you? If I have a sister, I'm gonna want to know her. If you're anywhere near

Jersey, we have to meet. Was it when he was in the service, in Oklahoma? Did he know about you? Did he ever have any contact with you? Does my mom know? This is like life changing stuff here, you're going to have to give me a lot more information."

As I read his responses, I could feel his agitation. It was understandable; he'd just found out that his father had another child and never mentioned it. I'm sure it happens all the time but it's still a major shock when it's *your* father.

"OMG" I replied. "I'm so sorry. When you didn't ask why I was looking for him I just assumed you already knew. Yes, he knew about me, and so did you mother. I was born in 1960 and I have no idea if your parents were married at that time"

"No, they didn't marry until 1962... I am shocked beyond words" he wrote.

My eyes kept going back to one of his statements: *"If I have a sister, I am going to want to know her."*

"My mother was only nineteen when I was born. I met him once, when I was about fifteen," I responded. "He said he would keep in touch with me, but he didn't. I didn't try to contact him after that, because he knew where I was and he chose not to contact me. Now I am crying because you said you want to meet me." I had so many emotions going through me at that moment. I was a mess.

"I really thought you knew. The casual way you just answered me made me think you did. I live in the Bronx and have three children. My mother's first cousin Barbara kept in touch with your mom." I guessed that he needed some time to digest all of this information so I stopped there.

"You're going to have to give me a minute to wrap my head around all of this," he wrote. "And of course I want to meet you. I'm trying to figure out how to confirm this is true. Not that I don't believe you, but you could be a loon for all I know. I don't want to talk to my Mom until I'm certain she knows. So now I have to go to Boston." I sat there, and wondered what I would do in his place.

"I am fairly certain she knows," I wrote. "I had cancer five years ago, and Barbara spoke to your mother to see if there was any family history. Also, my mother knew that your mother was in Boston, so I am guessing she was living there then. I hope you don't mind my saying because I don't know anything about your mother, but I know she didn't want you to know about me. I've been a secret for more than 50 years, so she may not react well. Do you have an aunt or an uncle you could ask first? Or start by asking if she remembers the name Barbara Bligh. My mother is Frances Reith. I really am sorry... I don't want anything except to know about him, and you."

"Ok, I believe you," he wrote. "I'm not upset, I'm even kind of a little excited; it's a revelation. The ramifications are too much to ponder just yet, but more family is always good :) I don't know where to go from here. Did he know about you when your mom was pregnant or were you a surprise at fifteen? I have go see my Mom and sister. This is not a phone conversation. I gave the eulogy at the funeral, I'll try and attach it, that's a start. After I gave it everyone was after me to write all his old stories down, but I can't seem to get around to it. This certainly gives it a new hook though. I'll go see my Mom and sister Mother's day weekend and get back to you after that. I don't feel right meeting you until I've spoken to them. I don't know, it's kind of confusing emotionally. I'll get back to you, I promise." We exchanged email addresses so he could send the eulogy. " I have so many questions," he wrote.

"Was he asked to stay out of your life when you were a child? Did Your mom marry, was there a dad in the house at all? I'm trying to find something to assuage the shame that I feel on his behalf. Did you always know he was your dad? Do you have any siblings? Are you ok with the cancer thing? Is it over or still looming? Ok, that's enough for now. Have to retype the eulogy, it got lost in the last computer crash. I'm so sorry you had to find out about his passing in such a casual way. I thought you were an old friend trying to find him."

"I don't have all of the answers," I wrote back. "I don't think he was asked to stay out, but I don't know for sure. My mother gave me only crumbs of information over the years. I had a stepfather from the age of three, and a younger sister and brother. I always knew that my stepfather was not my father because my brother and sister have a different last name and I have my mom's maiden name. When you're little, that kind of thing matters. I was different. I used to ask my mother about my father a lot when I was small. She would give me little pieces of information and told me I was like him. He liked to tell stories and write, and I loved to write stories too. She even told me his name at some point."

"When I was fifteen, mom heard he was in the neighborhood and took me to see him. Unfortunately she didn't tell me that's what was happening, so I didn't know how to react at the time. Mom hoped meeting him would help me "get over it" somehow. In a sense she was right, I didn't look for him or ask about him after that. I figured he knew where I was if he wanted to see me. You have no reason to feel shame on his behalf. We certainly can't control what our parents did or didn't do. My mother wasn't happy to hear I'd found you on facebook. I am sure there are many confused emotions for her, like for you, and for your mother as well, I'm guessing."

"I am okay," I continued. "I finished treatment five years ago and am considered 'cured.' I worry about long term effects from the chemo, but hey, I figure I am here on borrowed time anyway. I almost didn't even tell you why I was looking for him. When you told me he'd passed, I was shocked because I realized I was too late. Then I didn't want to upset the applecart for you and your family. You said a sister, just the one? Or are there others?

"I wanted to talk to him, just once as an adult to tell him how I felt growing up and show him what he missed by not knowing me. I think I'm a good person, worth knowing. I wanted to tell him about the three grandchildren he never knew, and wanted to find out about him and his other children. I missed it; I waited too long. I asked where he was buried so I could go there and tell him that. You don't need to be sorry, I shocked you, too. I felt terrible contacting you at first, but now I'm glad. Just this exchange with you is cathartic. Too bad facebook wasn't around 40 years ago," I wrote. I did feel better after getting all of that out there.

TWO
SPIRITUAL BELIEFS

I am a medium; I can communicate with people who have died and are now in the spirit world. It is something that my soul has always known I could and should do, but my human self resisted until I was in my 50's. There were experiences throughout my life that I couldn't explain, but I pushed them to the side and ignored them. The tendency to ignore experiences that don't fit into our frame of reference is normal and it's called "psychic amnesia" because it's a coping mechanism. It's only now when I share my story I realize how many times I was given an opportunity to acknowledge that there is another world intimately connected with this one.

There is a God, and we are all connected and part of that Infinite Intelligence and creative force. There is so much more to life than what we see. We operate in connection with a higher energy and we can tap into that energy at will. Anything is possible. Once we realize this, we begin to discover who we are.

This knowledge opens our minds to unlimited possibilities and highlights our own limited beliefs so we can overcome them. We have to unlearn what we've been raised to believe about ourselves in order to understand and appreciate our potential. It is only when we do that, that we "remember" who we are and why we're here. I know that must sound a little crazy, but that's how it worked for me. In order to be whole in this life, you must know who you are and why you are here. Part of knowing who you are is knowing where you came from; your family. I didn't know my father.

My mother was just nineteen when I was born and he was out of her life before he knew that she was pregnant. Not knowing a parent is a hole in my identity. I believe that we need to know where we are from, in this life, to understand where we are going. Not knowing my father left me with large gaps. There are so many unanswered questions and it's hard to explain the way it feels. I know there are millions of people out there who understand what I mean. I'm also sure there are books written by psychologists and psychiatrists on this topic; this book is not one of them. I write only from my own experience.

Once we know who we are in this world, we can start to understand who we are in relation to the Infinite Intelligence that is God. When we understand our own soul, our purpose, we are finally on the spiritual path. The catch here is that we already know on a soul level, but our human self has forgotten.

Socialization has given us our identity. We believe the world's opinion of who we are. For example, I always believed that I was bad at math. When I was in first and second grade, I struggled to learn mathematical concepts.

Doing homework was a nightmare. The adults around me would get frustrated when they tried to help me. First, the language they used around numbers was different from what I was being taught in school. When I was using the term 'zero' the adults said 'aught.' I had no idea what they were talking about. I was frustrated and so were they.

I believed that math was "hard" and that I just didn't get it. That became a belief I held about myself into adulthood. It was a false belief, a limiting belief, but one that stayed with me for many years. I actually never learned the multiplication tables. We were supposed to figure out what 5X7 was, by counting groups of seven until we got the answer. It wasn't until I was teaching fifth grade that I memorized the times tables, and it made such a difference in my math confidence. I realized that many of my students also had not learned the multiplication tables and were struggling because they had to figure out the multiplication or division instead of just knowing the number facts. I bought a *multiplication rap* cassette tape, and made it part of our daily routine, to listen and rap the answers. We looked at the concepts on paper or the blackboard, and they became clear to all of my students. I learned right along with them.

We have to get past our limiting beliefs and unlearn what we've been taught to believe about ourselves because it simply isn't true. I believe that this world is soul school. Our souls have lived many lives, and are constantly evolving. Earth is the elementary school of the universe. The point of being here is to learn something. This is not an original concept; many have written about reincarnation and have added their own theories to the collective.

I believe, like others do, that we set up our life circumstances. We chose our parents, and the situation we were born into so we can learn. We are part of a soul group and reincarnate with other members of the group to play different roles for each other. Some stay spirit side, in order to monitor what those reincarnating are doing and assist when needed. There is a plan, however the concept of free will is part of the earth experience. Once here, we forget about the plan and don't remember that we're here for a reason. We have to fumble our way through without the memory or knowledge of why we are here. This life becomes our reality and we believe whatever we've been socialized to believe. We may or may not learn what we set out for, and we may have to start over again. What I know absolutely is that when this life is over, we don't cease to exist. We continue to live in another form and we retain our personalities and memories on the other side until we reincarnate again.

I have wondered how that is possible. How is it that we maintain our individual personalities and memories if reincarnation is true? How can a medium communicate with my grandmother if she has reincarnated and is living now as somebody else? Some believe in alternate realities, or different dimensions of existence which all operate at the same time. I have been taught that the concept of time in the spirit world is very different from time on earth. Some say that there is no "time" as we know it in the next life. Maybe we don't reincarnate until all of our immediate family is also on the other side. I certainly don't have all the answers. What I know for certain is that we continue to live after the change called death, and we can communicate with people in the spirit world. What I've learned is that our family and friends in the spirit world communicate with us even when we don't recognize it. They can still influence us in this life. That's why I wrote this book. I want you to know that it is never too late... It's never too late to recognize that you are part of a much larger whole. It's never too late for a spiritual awakening. It's never too late to talk with the people in your life who have already transitioned into the spirit world.

THREE
GETTING TO KNOW PAUL

Paul shared with me that he suffered from bipolar disorder. He struggled to describe the extreme highs and lows he experienced when he wasn't on his medication. He hated taking the medication, but knew he had to in order to maintain control. He had a son with autism who he loved more than life itself. His marriage, unfortunately, was dying. He'd been going through a pretty hard time when I contacted him. He'd worked in advertising and marketing and had been successful but had been laid off in the last recession. Paul realized that he'd hated going into the city, and was fed up with the corporate rat race. He decided that he didn't want to go back to his former career and wanted to explore other possibilities. He was trying on different occupations and knew that he wanted to work with his hands.

Fishing was Paul's passion. He absolutely loved being in a boat with a line in the water. It gave him a sense of freedom, and peace. In preparation for the holidays he went for blackfish which his extended family loved. He said he wanted to take me fishing when we could get together in person. I also learned from Paul that my father had owned a business erecting steel structures inside stores and warehouses. My brother and many of his friends spent summers working for our dad. He was a father figure for many of them, and they sometimes went to him rather than their own parents if they needed advice or got into trouble. He told me that my father had been in the air force. While he was in the service he had done some boxing under an assumed name. I accepted each piece of information as a gift, something precious he was sharing with me. We became close before we ever met in person; it was easy to love Paul. He was very genuine, honest and open with me and we just seemed to click. He emailed the eulogy to me, included here.

It's staggering when you first realize your parents' love for you while holding your child.

My Dad used to say, "Welcome to adulthood," to all new parents and I think he was right on many levels.

My Dad touched so many people, so many of my friends, my nephews, my cousins,

my wife,

my son....

Dad occupied that rare space between Grown-up and friend,

A "Grown-up With Privileges," if you will - and it was a privilege he enjoyed with so many of us that he steered to manhood.

A privilege he never took for granted.

So I'm sitting staring at the water, thinking about how to sum up my Father's life.

He was a tough Guinea from the Bronx

He was a writer

He was Ephram Ramirez, Prize-fighter ducking Strategic Air Command rules

He was a bartender with stories in both pockets and a hammer in his right hand, dispensed liberally as needed

He was lifelong friend to my Uncle Jerry and my cousin Steven's second Dad

He was jump-master on a plane that crash landed in the Arctic Circle

He was old school before it was cool

He was a competitor

He was witty and crude and insightful and funny

God he was funny — he saw the world sideways

He was strong

He was the charming scoundrel

He was Husband and Uncle,

Son and Brother......and finally Poppa

He was family

Always family

He was married to the same women for 45 years

He saw the beautiful spirit beneath the gang-girl tough and knew who he wanted to be mother to his children

He slept safe sure in her sincerity

He was affectionate and passionate and the reason I can still kiss my son

And why he kisses back, why we haven't lost him

He is permanent

He taught me honor

He took me fishing

He was proud of my sister and me, "roses that grew from garbage," he would say

It was never like that, we never had to worry about having a home – with Dad you could always come home

But mostly Dad was fierce

Fierce in his love for his family and friends

Fierce in his beliefs

Fierce in his loyalty

Fiercely protective

He lived his life fearlessly

He died still fighting

He use to say he was rich in the things that mattered – you all being here, and so many kind words, shows it to be true

I guess to sum up I'd say, for so many of us,

His is a memory writ LARGE....

After reading this I understood how much Paul loved, respected, and admired our father. While I was happy to learn about the man who fathered me, I was also struck by the irony of it all. Paul's father was fiercely protective of his family and was a father-figure to many of Paul's friends. "He was family, Always family" ...just not for me. How could the man Paul revered (with the qualities he attributed to him) be the same man who had walked away from me? My frank reaction to reading the eulogy was jealousy. Paul had the father I had always wanted — fiercely protective, affectionate, passionate and funny.

FOUR
DIFFICULT CONVERSATIONS

I nervously waited to hear from Paul after Mother's Day although I'd told my own family at Easter dinner. When I think about it now, I realize that I should've told my mother first. After dinner the whole family was sitting around talking; my children, mother, brother and his family, an aunt and a few of my first cousins and their families.

I don't remember the exact sequence of the conversation, but I hadn't intended on telling my family yet. My cousin Pete also wondered about his father throughout his life just like I had. His wife Franny had commented on this over the years and her compassion for his feelings was obvious. Somehow it all came up at dinner and Franny and Pete's mom got into an argument. It got heated, and my aunt left the party. I felt that Franny hadn't tried to see it from his mother's perspective. This didn't sit well with me, and I said so. Emotions were high at the table and this is when I decided to tell my family I'd found my brother.

I started by asking my mother for the maiden name of my father's wife, which Paul had mentioned in the very first private message between us. My mother gave me the same name, looking at me as if to ask why. I told them I'd looked on Facebook and found my brother. I gave them a summary of the conversation and the fact that he planned on telling his mother and sister on Mother's Day. My mother got quiet and didn't say much the rest of the night.

In the weeks that followed my mother told me that my father had been her first love. She said she wasn't the pretty one in her family and hadn't much experience with dating or men at the time. I heard the insecure teenager that she was as she talked about him. When they started seeing each other, it was exciting and new and she fell in love. She believed that he loved her too, and one thing led to another. My mother was raised Catholic and went to Catholic school as a girl. Having sexual relations outside of marriage was considered a sin.

She grew up with her cousins on her father's side of the family and they were part of a larger circle of friends. She had been out late with her cousin Barbara and friends and a few people went back to my aunt Barbara's house and crashed. Even though Barbara is my mothers' first cousin and not my aunt, I was taught to call her aunt, like I called all of her cousins. I also had aunts and uncles who were not blood relatives at all. Anyway, there weren't enough beds for everyone who needed one, and my mother ended up on one end of a sofa while one of the guys was on the other. At some point my father walked in and saw her sleeping on the sofa with some guy, and jumped to conclusions.

My mother explained that it was totally innocent, but he would hear none of it. That was it, their relationship was over. She couldn't convince him that she'd had no interest in the guy and just wanted to get some sleep. He walked away from her just like that. What neither of them knew at the time was that she was already pregnant with me.

Their relationship was completely over. He said that she could be pregnant with anybody's child and how could he know it was his? I was born in 1960 and they didn't have DNA testing then. My father was pretty hard about this if you ask me. He must have felt betrayed and hurt seeing my mother sleeping on the sofa with another man. I don't know enough about him to judge, but I wonder why he couldn't consider that my mother's explanation might be true?

I've come to understand he had a rough childhood himself and his family contributed to the hard outer shell he'd developed. His own father had died when he was a young boy, and his mother was left with him and his sister to raise alone. She remarried and had another son with her new husband, but things were not easy. Her new husband was abusive and as a boy my father watched this relationship until he was old enough to get out on his own.

At the age of eighteen my mother faced her parents and told them she was pregnant. Her father was an alcoholic and was abusive. I know that they did not react well to the news. I don't know exactly what happened or what was said, but I know my mother left her parent's house. It was 1960 and women were pushed to give their babies up for adoption after living in a home for unwed mothers during their pregnancy. She eventually returned with me in tow.

FIVE
PAVING THE WAY

Before I discovered mediumship I just drifted along. I went to Lehman College in the Bronx because it was close to home. I majored in mass communication and public speaking and graduated cum laude and with departmental honors in both majors.

I sat for the LSAT entrance exam for law school. It was a bad morning and I woke up late, quickly threw clothes on and drove to the testing site. I was discombobulated, and my scores reflected that. I bombed my test and then I gave up on the idea of law school. I probably should have studied and taken the test again, but I didn't believe I was smart enough to be a lawyer.

I met my husband pretty soon after. He was funny and my family loved him. After we married I found a job as an office worker/secretary in the New York City office of a textile mill. I worked there for a year and heard about a job as a paralegal working for large corporations. It was boring but I did well there until I got pregnant with my first child. After I had my son Anthony I resigned. I started taking education courses at night. I eventually earned a certificate that allowed me to substitute teach. I had been about to take the exam for licensing when I discovered that I was pregnant again and decided to postpone it. I had another son Daniel.

The state board later changed the requirements and I had to take a whole different set of exams for my teaching license. My husband Sal was a drummer in a band and taught music in a parochial school. His weekends were late nights playing with his band, and I was home with the boys. I was stressed and our bills were piling up. Sal used most of his gig money to buy new drums and recording equipment instead of what was needed for our family of four. The parochial school salary was low, but we did have health insurance.

I started tending bar in a small beach club a couple days a week while my in-laws watched the kids. I was making pretty good money, but a drinking lifestyle was the norm, even for the staff.

While my husband and I already had two boys, we got pregnant one more time and had a little girl. I worked behind the bar right up to a month before she was born although I didn't drink at that time of course. Someone always helped me lift the heavy stuff.

We were living in a one bedroom co-op apartment and I wanted a small house, but Sal didn't want to move. I started saving part of what I made tending bar. It was that money that put me into my first apartment when I did leave when my daughter was around two years old. Sal is a good man and a great father, but we were not very good together. He had started teaching in the public schools by then, and earning a better income. We went to marriage counseling for a time, but by then my mind was made up and there was no way to save the marriage, which I felt was already over. I told the counselor straight off that I was there to figure out how to least impact our children in our breakup. They were impacted, of course, and I felt guilty about that for years.

After I had my daughter Lauren I started subbing in the public school system. Students challenge substitutes every minute of the day to see what they can get away with, and it's a hard job. I was not a fan of subbing and it wasn't helping me get my teaching certification. I needed to do a year of student teaching without pay, or teach in a parochial school. I took a job in a parochial school which gave me a small income. It was basically learning on the go, and the worst part was that I was expected to teach religion. My knowledge of the Catholic faith was basic, and I had to study the teacher's guide. We had to take our class to mass on Friday each week, and I had to fake the responses and motions. I felt like an imposter and worried that someone would discover this and I would be fired. However, I made it through the year and obtained a job in the public school system.

The point of all of this is to say that I really never figured out what I wanted to be when I grew up. I decided on teaching because it would be convenient for me as a mother. It was not my passion, and though I was proficient and eventually good at it, I didn't love it. It provided me with an income and health benefits. I had no long term plans to get to retirement other than to get to retirement. My circumstances are what decided my goals. I found pleasure in escaping, reading novels, going out with friends or hanging out at the club. I had no real interests or skills, and no passion for life. I gave up whenever anything was too hard. I almost quit teaching because of an especially challenging fifth grade class one year, but didn't because I needed to pay the bills. I was going back to school to get a master's degree in education so I could keep my teaching job. I was like millions of other people who worked to survive.

I taught at a small elementary school in the Bronx for ten years. I found it very challenging my first few years planning lessons and reading professional books and had time for little else. After a few years I got more comfortable and actually started to like it. I went into the profession for all the wrong reasons, but found I was good at it. I wanted to be involved in the decisions that shaped our school, and sat on the School Leadership Team. I was all about the kids, how we could educate them and help shape them into productive people. After a while, however, I wondered why the teachers were not respected or valued. I went to our union representative and told her that I wanted to be more involved with the union. She was thrilled to hear it, and started giving me little responsibilities to help her out. When she was hired to work for the union full-time, I stepped in and was elected as chapter leader, which is what the shop steward is called in the schools. I found this new role both exciting and challenging.

The union sent me to different trainings, and one was on arbitration. This was a four-part training on weekends spread over the school year. I did very well and the instructors took an interest in me. I was hired to work after school in the central grievance department in lower Manhattan. Those were tough days. I would leave school to go park my car near the train, then headed downtown. I never got there before 4:30 and would end up staying until 7 or 8 pm trying to catch up on the work. So much for being home with my children. But they were teenagers by then and could manage without me for the most part. I worked like this for a year and then the following summer I was offered a full-time job. I was thrilled and excited at the opportunity.

The work suited me; reading and interpreting contract language satisfied my earlier desire to go to law school. I was able to use the communication skills I studied in college and I understood teachers since I had been one for ten years. I used my creativity to write opening and closing statements to persuade the arbitrator to see the case my way. I was earning more money than I had teaching. I finally felt like my life was coming together nicely. For the most part I enjoyed the people I worked with. I became friends with the woman who had been in charge of the training and was pretty happy in spite of the time commitment. I worked from 10 am to 6 pm daily, and it took me at 90 minutes to get to the union central headquarters from my home in the Bronx.

My opponents at arbitrations were all attorneys and even though I had never gone to law school, I was a good advocate. I won more cases than I lost and earned a good reputation. By the time I was working for the union as an arbitration advocate, I felt like I finally found something I was really good at. I enjoyed helping teachers and other school staff when they had issues with the system. I was making a difference until the politics of the job took me out of arbitrations and into grievances.

I was trained to represent teachers at u-rating appeals while I was still teaching. Coincidently, the year I was hired full-time the representation for those appeals was moved to the grievance department. Since the grievance staff had little to no experience with rating appeals, the director at the time made me responsible for them. I was also in charge of training new advocates to represent members at those appeals. The evaluation system changed about six or seven years later. Certain classes of teachers would now be rated *developing*, *effective*, or *ineffective*, while some teachers and other school staff were still rated under the older evaluation system.

This was a big shift because under the new system standardized test scores of students would be factored into the evaluations. The new system came with new appeals, including a new appeal for teachers who believed that their rating was based on harassment or something other than their classroom performance. I was asked to start a small subdivision of the grievance department to focus on evaluation appeals. While the other appeals were heard by representatives of the Department of Education, these appeals would be heard by a neutral arbitrator.

I spent the next couple of years working exclusively on appeals, with the major focus on the harassment appeals. We actually won a good number of these which many people thought would be impossible. The president of the union decided that we didn't need a subdivision for appeals anymore, and they were folded back into the responsibilities of the central grievance department. I was reassigned to the Bronx borough office to do grievances. I was not happy about this.

I felt like I had been demoted. I had worked my ass off creating processes for the new evaluation system and then actually winning harassment cases against all odds. I felt like they were throwing me away. I was humiliated and depressed when the move was finalized. I wondered how I would be able to hold my head up with the other staff at the union who would certainly be wondering what I had done to be ousted from central this way. I was meditating by this time as a regular practice. I was using guided meditations and began listening to those with self-esteem, confidence, and gratitude themes.

There were some positives to this new assignment. First, the office was only six minutes away from my home by car, and they had a large parking lot. I would no longer spend three hours every day commuting. This financial advantage also saved the costs of my commute which were significant. More importantly, I would have more time every day. I imagined in that extra hour and a half in the morning I could join a gym. My official work hours were 10 am until 6 pm, but I often worked until 8 and sometimes 9 pm, depending on what cases were coming and what needed to be done. I brought work home too, sometimes working on the weekends. Doing grievances meant I wouldn't be doing arbitrations. I wouldn't always have a case hanging over my head, and I probably would not have to work on weekends or when I got home anymore.

It was starting to sound better and better to me. I adjusted pretty quickly, deciding that it was the Union's loss and my gain. I stopped worrying about what other people thought. Let them think what they wanted to. I have to credit the meditations with the speed of my adjustment. I started to see the move as a blessing, and indeed it was. It allowed me to take my focus off work and explore other avenues of interest. It gave me the opportunity to begin the development of my mediumship.

SIX
MEDITATION

In the years before I was transferred to the Bronx, I was under a lot of stress. The work itself was stressful, and the friend I had made became the new director of the department and my boss. That was not working out well. I started getting frequent migraine headaches and was not a happy camper.

The headaches became so bad that I went to see a neurologist. I had an MRI of my brain and surprise... they found a small tumor, called a meningioma, over the frontal lobe. The tumor was not in my brain, but in the material that covers it. The neurologist assured me that this was not the cause of my headaches, and there was nothing that needed to be done other than monitoring it. As a cancer survivor, I wanted a second opinion and I wanted an authority. I contacted my oncologist at Memorial Sloan Kettering Hospital who got me an appointment with a neurologist there. After taking additional MRIs this doctor agreed with the first: this wasn't causing the headaches, and just had to be monitored. He suggested that it was the stress of my job causing the headaches, and told me I needed to meditate. Meditate? Really? The word conjured up images of the Buddha and contorted positions I had no desire to assume.

"Really" he assured me. "Just try it, you can even use an app on your phone, but you need to start now" he said.

I went home and installed a meditation app on my phone, thinking it was not going to help at all. Since I had a 90 minute commute to work each day, I thought the bus ride would be a good time to try this out. I used guided meditations to start, and didn't notice anything right away. After a few weeks, however, I felt happier. I noticed that I was dealing with the stress differently. I was more relaxed, the headaches decreased and eventually disappeared. I couldn't believe it, but it worked. I used all types of guided meditations at the time, for confidence, happiness, self-esteem; you name it, I tried it. And the end result was really amazing. I was happier, more confident, less stressed, etc. There were other effects as well.

One particular morning as I was looking for a new meditation, I saw one about visiting a departed loved one. My grandmother had passed years before, and I missed her terribly. She had been a huge part of my life as a child, as I had grown up in her house along with assorted aunts, uncles and an occasional stray. So, I played that meditation. It started like all the others, with instructions to relax, follow my breathing, etc. Meditations like this actually bring you into an altered state of mind, similar to being in hypnosis. I was told to envision myself sitting on a bench, in a park. There were trees all around and large expanses of beautiful green grass. I could hear the birds chirping, the sun was shining and occasionally someone would walk by and say hello.

Next, I was told to imagine my loved one approaching from behind me.

I could feel the energy of my grandmother, Nan, behind me at this point. She came and sat next to me on the bench. I was already crying, but I wrapped my arms around her and told her how much I missed her. We held hands; I told her how sorry I was that I hadn't visited her much before she passed. She had dementia for several years before she died. She told me it was all right; she was fine now and loved me very much. It was over too fast. The meditation was telling me to say goodbye, but I didn't want to. When it was over, I was a puddle and trying not to sob out loud on the bus. It had seemed so real. I mused over it all day. Could it have been real? I actually felt her there with me. No, it wasn't likely. I decided that the meditation was designed to make me feel like it was real, and it had done its job. I promptly put it out of my mind.

SEVEN

SEEING SPIRITS

As a little girl, I hated the dark. I shared a bed with my sister for some time when we were young. Jane was four years younger than I was. We lived in my grandmother's house which had two floors. The upstairs was set up as a separate apartment, with an old kitchen. There were only three rooms; the kitchen, a small middle room, and a bedroom at the back. It had lots of windows and the corners were rounded like turrets. I loved that room because it made me feel like I was in a castle. My mother painted it pink and put pretty flowery wallpaper on two walls. Bob, my sister's father, had built a big open closet along one wall with no doors. At night I was always afraid of the shadows and shapes in every rounded corner. The shadows looked like people with dour, angry faces. I would squeeze my eyes shut tight or pull the covers over my head to ignore them. I never thought about trying to talk to them. I was just afraid.

I wonder now if I was seeing spirit or if it was my young imagination running wild or maybe a bit of both. When I was really afraid, or when I had a bad dream and woke up in the middle of the night, I would sometimes gather up the courage to get out of bed and run downstairs to tell my mother. If she was home she would tell me to go back to bed, that there was nothing to be afraid of. Then I would go find my grandmother who I called Nanny. She would simply move over and I would hop into her bed. She never told me to go back to my own bed. It wasn't long before I skipped going to my mother and went straight to Nanny's bed. I can still remember curling up against her, and feeling entirely safe with her.

I remember that there were still aunts and uncles living at home when I was small. My aunt Liz slept in the middle room upstairs. My uncle Pete still lived there too. I don't exactly know where he slept. My uncle Donald did not officially live there as he had a family and lived in Queens. However, he would show up unannounced and stay for periods of time. Aunt Claire was married and didn't live in the house. Nana had five children: Donald, Frances, Claire, Peter and Elizabeth, in that order. Frances is my mother. Since my mother was nineteen when I was born, I guess it makes sense that some of them were still living home when I was a child. There was lots of extended family living in the area where we lived. It was a small community and I had relatives on practically every block. My grandfather's family all lived in the same area. His sisters and brother all had houses, and their children, who were my mother's first cousins, all lived there too. It was both a blessing and a curse to grow up with so much family nearby. No matter where I went in the neighborhood someone knew me, and it was very likely a relative.

EIGHT
WISHING FOR A FATHER

I used to spend hours daydreaming about my father when I was a child. In my mind he was kind and loving and treated me like a little princess. I spent time with my imaginary father when I wasn't happy with my actual family, or when I was in trouble for something.

I was different from the kids in my neighborhood who lived with two parents, a mother and father. I had a grandmother, mother, and aunts and uncles. I envied the kids who lived in "normal" family units because they only had two people in charge of them, while I had an entire group.

My aunt might tell me to do one thing while my uncle told me another. I was both fascinated and nervous around the fathers of the other children, and uneasy with adult men in general. I used to worry about the silliest things as I grew up like who would give me away at my wedding?

As a young adult when I was getting married, I provided my baptismal certificate to the church. It had something written in the place for my father's name but I couldn't figure out what it said. I stressed over it and worried about it. When my fiancé and I met with the priest, I presented my certificate and told him that I had no idea what the written phrase meant. He chuckled and said it was latin for "ignore this." I didn't think it was very amusing. In fact, I was embarrassed. Every time I saw a doctor and they wanted a family history I would have to explain that I didn't know about my father. He was a gaping hole in my identity, medically and socially.

I had several father figures in my life. My uncle Peter, who could be stern and scary sometimes, but was usually good to me. He occasionally took me on an outing, to Rockaway once and to the zoo another time. He used to yell at me, my sister and cousins when they were in the house to put our slippers on. We all remember that about him to this day. I loved being barefoot, and during the summer I hardly ever wore anything on my feet, inside or outside. It was part of growing and most of the kids in the neighborhood went barefoot in the summer. My uncle always insisted there be something on my feet.

My mother's partner Bob was the father of my sister Jane and brother Tommy. I only ever called him Bob; never anything else. He would occasionally round up all the neighborhood kids and take us all to the drive-in movies. He was generous and would buy us ice cream when the truck came down the block for anyone who was around.

Bob also had a couple of older daughters. One of his daughters knew a girl from our neighborhood but we weren't friends. I remember when I was in junior high she told me she knew Debbie and asked how I was related. I said she was my step-sister because it seemed the easiest thing to say. Not long after I saw Debbie and she let me know that she was not my step sister, that I was nothing to her, and that I'd better not go around saying anything different.

Another father figure in my life was Uncle Bobby, who was married to my Aunt Barbara. He loved the fact that I would try any food as a child. They took me out to eat and fed me scungilli and calamari and other foods I didn't usually have. Before Aunt Barbara had a child of her own, she told my mom that Bobby loved me so much she was afraid that he wouldn't love his own kids as much as he loved me. He was sweet to me. Aunt Barbara had a number of miscarriages before she finally gave birth to their first child, Robert. She needn't have worried, of course. Uncle Bobby remained a big part of my life and was the person who eventually walked me down the aisle at my wedding.

When I was fifteen or so, my mother heard my father was visiting a neighborhood tavern. She told me to get into her car but she wouldn't tell me where we were going or why. As we neared the place, she told me that my father was there and she wanted me to meet him. It wasn't the most opportune time as my best friend and I had been experimenting with pot and I was pretty stoned. It would be an understatement to say it was an awkward night.

I was introduced to this stranger, my father, in a bar. It was obvious that he had known about me but there was no conversation about what happened or why. Finally when it was time to go I sat outside with him in his car for a few minutes while my mother sat in hers. I don't know why my mother thought this was a good idea or what she thought he was going to say. She thought it would be healing for me in some way but he looked uncomfortable and didn't know what to say other than he'd thought about me a lot over the years. He asked for my phone number and promised he would be in touch. I never heard from him again.

I was angry with him after that. I decided that he'd had an opportunity to get to know me and he'd thrown it away. I was hurt, and I buried that hurt in anger. I decided that he wasn't worth knowing and that it was his loss. I had grown up all right without him. Looking back I remember that my grandmother always said I didn't need him anyway. If I asked her about him, she would say he died in the war, and change the subject. After meeting him, I decided that she was right.

I was a rebellious teenager and my relationship with my mother was strained in these years. I left home for the first time when I was in middle school. I went to Norwalk Connecticut to stay with Aunt Chickie and Uncle Matty. They had six children, a big house, and an in-ground swimming pool in the yard. I thought the place was like a mansion. I always loved Aunt Chickie. She was magical to me and called me her "fellow Leo" as we were both born in August. She has the most wonderful laugh and sense of humor. She laughed at herself often and had no qualms about admitting she was a bit ditzy at times. Her three oldest children were boys, born a year or two apart so she had her hands full for sure.

The school system was better than the public schools I attended in the Bronx. My mother wanted what was best for me, and I was all for it. I imagined myself living in that huge house with my cousins and that big swimming pool, and thought it would be wonderful. I transferred to the school in Connecticut and slept in the family room off of the kitchen. I was excited to be there, but in for a bit of culture shock. I had no experience being with so many other kids at meal times. If you weren't quick you'd still be hungry.

Matty was maybe a year older than me, then there was Kirk who was a year younger than me. My cousin Chris was next in line, then came Mary, Robin and later, Paul. I grew up with them as part of my extended family. I remember Aunt Chickie telling the story of how Matty and Kirk had covered Chris in black shoe polish while he was in his crib. She said she walked in and saw him lying there, and thought he had been burnt to ashes, laughing as she told the story.

My cousins were both fun and annoying. While they were sharing rooms upstairs, I had a room to myself downstairs. I wasn't used to the teasing or the mayhem. At school I felt like an outsider. The kids heard I was from the Bronx and asked me ridiculous questions like had I ever been mugged, or seen a lot of shootings? Most of them only knew the Bronx portrayed on television as drug infested and gang saturated. I made a couple of friends, but wanted to go home. I finished out the year and transferred back to my junior high school in the Bronx.

The next time I left home was when I was in high school. I stayed with a former teacher I became friends with. I stayed a couple of months and then went back home. After high school I drove down to Florida for a week, but stayed the entire summer. I got a waitress job and lived with my cousins before deciding to go home and go to college.

NINE
UNEXPLAINED EXPERIENCES

I did have some strange experiences growing up. I remember my cousins and I taking turns jumping off the stairs in my grandmother's house. The stairs were steep and very narrow; we started on the bottom, working our way up one at a time. I was barely five or six, and I was the oldest of them. I deliberately went up to the top step and jumped. I should have been hurt, I should have broken a bone or something. Instead, I floated down in slow motion, landing with a thump on my bottom.

I know that people are not going to believe it, but it is a memory that remains clear in my mind. I sat there in wonder, trying to figure out what had just happened. I don't remember any of my cousins noticing. I was the only one. I knew it wasn't normal and knew that someone or something had just protected me from my own stupidity. I thought maybe I had a fairy godmother, like Cinderella. While my family was technically Catholic, we were not practicing Catholics. However, after floating down the stairs, I knew in my heart that there was definitely something protecting me.

DIANE FRANCES

I was always interested in psychic phenomena, which used to be called "the occult." Psychics were very popular in the 70s and I was fascinated by them. I saw a show where a psychic was tested with cards that had shapes on them. While watching, I guessed the shapes at the same time but I didn't do very well. When I was twelve or thirteen I bought a deck of Tarot cards. I loved reading. It was always my favorite thing to do. I read that these cards should be kept in a wooden box, no metal on them. I couldn't figure out where to buy a box like this.

There was a small carpentry shop in my neighborhood, where they built furniture and things out of wood. I went there and told the man that I needed a small box, and gave him one of those information cards that came with the deck. I told him no metal, just all wood. I asked that my name be put on top of the box. He told me it would be ready in a couple of days and I paid him. I don't remember what it cost, but I had the money for it. When I went back, I was not happy, because he had put small metal hinges on the top of the box, to hold it to the bottom. But I took the box anyway, and put my cards in it.

I bought a paperback book on Tarot and read it cover to cover. Then I would shuffle for myself and do layouts, going to the book for every card. After a bit my family started asking me to read their cards. I read for my aunt by the book, and I could tell by her reactions that I had hit on a few things. She started laughingly referring to me as a "witch." Unfortunately, I never got too much farther than that with Tarot. I kept the cards but didn't use them often. If I was under some kind of stress in those years, I would pull them out and read for myself, then promptly forget all about them. Now I understand that Tarot cards have traditional meanings, but should really be read intuitively as a psychic tool.

As a teenager, I hung out with a large group of kids. One girl's family moved upstate and her mother let her invite a bunch of us up for the weekend. Not everyone went, but it was still a large group that descended upon their house. We didn't need much in the way of entertainment; there was always something going on and the weekend was a blast. This was in the 70's and the singer, Jim Croce, had recently passed. Someone suggested we have a seance, and try to get Jim Croce. A group of us were willing to try.

I acted as the medium asking the spirits to bring Jim Croce to us, while the others sat with me in a circle in the large living room, allegedly concentrating on being open to the spirit world. We were a bunch of kids with no idea what we were doing and it was exciting and silly at the same time. After a while I could feel the atmosphere in the room change and it became more serious. I continued asking for the spirit to join us when the room became colder. My best friend, Liz, started to talk in the voice of a man. I don't remember exactly what she said, but everyone was freaked out. A few people got up and ran out of the room into the kitchen and that promptly ended our seance. The lights were turned on and there was a lot of nervous laughter. Liz didn't remember any of it and we had to tell her what had happened. There were no more seances after that.

As a young adult, I didn't have very many experiences with psychic phenomena. I always felt like I knew things about people, but can't specifically say what. I would get a "feeling" about various people. When I met someone for the first time, the feeling I got about them guided me as to whether I wanted to get to know them or not. While driving, I always seemed to know which car was going to change lanes without signaling. I think most people get feelings or knowings like this and don't think much of it. If I stopped to think about any of the feelings at the time I decided it was my imagination or that I was either crazy or judgmental. I convinced myself that I should stop paying attention to those feelings. What I know now is that these feelings are part of our intuition and psychic senses. They can be developed and expanded intentionally, but I didn't recognize that until much later in my life.

I did sometimes get information from dreams, however. When I was nineteen I dreamed that I was changing a baby girl in the small bedroom upstairs in my aunt Barbara's house. At the time, she had three sons and no plans to have another baby. Liz and I used to babysit for the boys when she and Uncle Bobby went out. I also spent time with her, sitting in her kitchen drinking coffee and talking about whatever. When I told her about the dream, she brushed it off with a laugh, saying she was too old to have any more babies. Then, a few weeks later, she told me that she was pregnant. She had a healthy baby girl when I was twenty, and asked me to be her godmother.

When I was in my 30's and married with two beautiful young boys, I was taking advantage of their nap time to take a nap myself. I was laying on the sofa in the living room while the boys slept in the single bedroom of our small apartment. I dreamed about a beautiful little girl, who would grow up to be an important person in my life.

I knew she would be my daughter. I didn't know at the time that I was pregnant, and frankly, my marriage was not doing well. When I realized that I was pregnant, I didn't tell anyone about the dream. It seemed too precious to share and I thought I would jinx it if I did.

My mother had decided that this baby would be a boy. "You're carrying the same way" she'd said, and everyone agreed. But I knew differently. It had been my secret. A secret I'd carried cupped in my hands, ever so gently, not wanting to share it and risk spoiling the magic it held.

I thought back to the day more than a year earlier. Anthony was at nursery school and I'd just put Danny down for a nap. I loved these two more than words could express. I was tired and lay down on the sofa thinking I would nap for a while myself. I slept for a time. I started to wake slowly, not quite aware of where I was.

I was in that place between dreaming and waking and I didn't want to leave it. I wanted to remain there, in the wonder of her presence. I knew her, could feel her, and we were happy. I grasped the remains of the dream, trying to hold it and keep it with me as long as I could. I didn't see her face, and had no clear vision of her in my mind. I did feel her in my heart, I felt her presence. I woke, regretfully, keenly feeling a sense of loss.

It was now a crisp and sunny January afternoon. How strange to bear a child in the middle of the day. The boys were born when babies should be, in the hours just before dawn. This was to be my third child, and would certainly be my last.

"Ok, now push" says the doctor from his perch at my feet. He catches her smoothly and whisks her onto her side to clear her airway.

"Congratulations Mommy! You have a beautiful little girl" he says, but I haven't heard her cry.

I hold my breath and crane my neck, struggling to see her, the panic rising up. Then I hear it, and I breathe. I shuddered as I eyed the huge knot in the cord that bound her to me still.

"Thank you, God," I say, relieved that she is here and not tangled up in there, the way her cousin was. Then finally I am holding her. I recognize her immediately. Her face holds the history of our family. My mother's eyes, her father's lips. In her face I can see my brother, and my sons. I would know her anywhere. In that instant I know that no matter what else might happen, this is right. This was meant to be, and I am truly blessed.

"We have a girl!" he shouted as Sal went to the waiting room. My mother got so excited, and then she punched him in the arm.

"Stop it. Don't play around with me." She thought he was joking. He had to tell her that he was serious, and that we really had a girl. My mother was so excited and thrilled. They let her come in to see me and she was laughing and crying at the same time. She told me that she hadn't believed it when Sal had told her. I knew she was excited because she didn't know what to do with herself.

Another strange thing happened to me during the years when I was still married. I was sleeping and felt like I was waking up. I suddenly felt a presence right next to me. I felt like someone was there, leaning on the side of the bed; I physically felt the pressure on the bed of a person standing there. I opened my eyes and saw the figure of a woman. She wasn't someone I knew and was dressed in rather old-fashioned clothing. It scared me, and I jolted and sat up. She instantly disappeared, but I couldn't shake the feeling that I'd seen someone. I didn't understand it, and it didn't happen again that I recall until much later in my life.

After my husband and I split up I moved into a small apartment near my mother, but I really wanted to live in a house. My mother worked with several attorneys who specialized in elder care. She had worked in a hospital previously and learned how to do medicaid and medicare applications for patients so that the hospital would be able to get paid when a patient didn't have insurance. She found that the skills she had learned there were in demand by elder care attorneys. In her work, she met many elderly people who she became friendly with and also met their families sometimes. I had been looking at houses in the small community I grew up in, but didn't really want to live there as an adult. Most houses in the surrounding area were too expensive for a new teacher's salary. I also did not have any money for a down payment.

My mother heard about a house in the area that was about to go on the market. The woman who owned it had recently passed, and her family wanted to sell it. She told the family that I was looking, and asked if we could see it. It needed lots of work, but I knew it was right for me. My mother loaned me the down payment and some money to start doing some of the work it needed, and I enlisted my brother Tom to get it done. I spent twenty years in that house and it was a blessing to me and my family.

Since discovering my mediumship and psychic abilities, I still have days where I just "know" things. When my children were grown and had all moved out, I thought many times about selling the house. The thought of clearing it out was pretty overwhelming. I had an attic, basement and two car garage which were all full of things. Many of them belonged to my children; old bicycles, sports equipment, clothes, dolls, pieces of furniture one of us hated to get rid of. I didn't think I was capable of doing it all, so I mainly ignored it by redecorating two of the upstairs bedrooms. One became a guest room in time for Liz to visit. I emptied it, repainted and ordered a new bed on Amazon. I also had a new baby granddaughter, so I turned the other bedroom into a space for her. I lived alone for a few years and then one day I woke up and knew it was time to sell. I called a realtor and listed that day. It took months to get everything in order, but it was being shown the whole time. We had a couple of people interested in it, but they hadn't panned out.

One family came to look, a couple with a son and younger daughter. It was one of the few times I was home when the house was shown to prospective buyers. When they came in, I greeted them and told the little girl that there was a room upstairs I thought she'd like. They made an offer on the house. There was some back and forth on price, and a few times I thought the deal would fall through. I remember waking up one morning to the song "Everything's Coming Up Roses." A few days later, upon waking I heard a voice say to me: "It's Marianna's house now." The deal was closed and they bought the house.

TEN

MEETING THE TEST

When I next heard from Paul it was in an email, and he copied our sister Dawn for the first time.

He told me that he'd spoken to his mother and Dawn, and they thought it would be a good idea if we took a sibling DNA test. I agreed immediately.

The next email was from Dawn. She wrote that she was glad that I was willing to take the test because she was still reeling from the information that Paul had given them. I would take a swab from the inside of my cheek and put in the specimen bottle, and mail it back to Dawn. Then she would add her specimen and one from her mother, who had agreed to take the test also. It seems it is better to have the DNA of at least one parent, to make it easier to differentiate between the potential siblings. When the packet came from Dawn I was both excited and anxious. I was excited that we would finally have proof that what I already knew was true but anxious about the potential that my mother might have been wrong. I know that it was my own monkey mind running wild because I already knew deep inside that we were siblings.

In my next conversation with Paul he said his mother had been upset when he told her I'd contacted him. He didn't give me many of the details, but the fact that Carol was willing to take the DNA test was a good sign. After several weeks the results were posted on the company website. For sibling DNA, a test result of .05 could indicate a sibling. The higher the score, the more likely and definite that we were siblings. Our score was 9.5 and I exhaled a huge breath once I'd seen the results. I was more nervous than I thought about the possibility that I was wrong and that my mother was wrong. I do feel bad about that because I should have trusted my intuition and the knowledge from the moment I saw Paul's Facebook profile. I could have saved myself all that anxiety. Also, I should have trusted my mother. She had told me that my father was the first person she'd ever been with, and she hadn't been with anyone else before my birth.

I emailed Dawn after reading the results.

"Based on everything I read on the site, I would say that this result is pretty conclusive. What do you think?" Dawn and Paul must have been talking between themselves quite a bit at this time.

I got an email from Paul and he was excited. He said he thought the test must be wonderful validation for my mother, and that she must feel vindicated. While I knew Paul only meant well, there was something about the word "vindicated" that bothered me. My mother wasn't trying to prove what she already knew.

My response to Paul was tempered. I didn't question his use of the word.

"My mother has always known. It's you and I who now know for sure."

Dawn emailed that she agreed the test was pretty conclusive. When we talked on the phone I was in my bedroom so I wouldn't be disturbed by anyone. It was one of those awkward conversations where you are trying to connect with someone but you're not sure how to go about it. It was a fragile new relationship and we were cautious. I asked her to send a photo of herself and we talked about our families, jobs, and things we liked to do. Dawn suggested that the three of us should meet. Paul was in New Jersey and Dawn was up in Boston, so we decided to meet somewhere in the middle. Paul booked three rooms at a hotel in Stamford CT so we were all across state lines. We planned to meet at the bar on that Saturday afternoon.

Packing for that trip made me panic because I didn't know what to wear or what to bring. I wasn't sure if I should dress up or be casual. Once I got to the hotel I stayed in my room fretting for a while.

When the time finally arrived to meet at the bar, I couldn't believe how nervous I was. Although she had sent me two pictures of herself after we'd spoken on the phone, I wasn't sure I'd recognize Dawn. When I walked into the hotel bar there were a few people seated but I didn't know anyone and took a seat. In Paul's Facebook photo he was on a fishing boat holding up a fish. He was also wearing a hat as he was in most of his online photos, and seemed a little heavy-set to me. I ordered a beer, and told the bartender that I was supposed to meet my brother for the first time, right here at this bar. Paul, who was sitting not very far away, looked up. He got out of his chair and walked towards me.

"Diane?"

It was emotional. We hugged and I said "I expected you to be bigger" referring to his weight, as he was not heavy at all. His response cracked me up and broke the tension.

"If I only had a nickel for every time I've heard that," he said. I laughed and then Dawn came in and walked over to us. We hugged a little awkwardly and the nervousness was palpable. We sat and made small talk and Paul had made a dinner reservation at a pub nearby. We had another drink and talked about our children and what they were doing. We walked to the pub feeling a little more comfortable and I recognized that they were similar to my own family and friends; they enjoyed telling stories from the past and having a few laughs. Paul asked me if I played pool. I had played once or twice but didn't really understand the game.

"I'll teach you," he said.

Dawn told me that they both liked to play and that our father had taught them when they were younger. We played for a couple of hours and had a few laughs. I was a terrible pool player and Paul had his work cut out for him. We were feeling comfortable together and we went back to the hotel lounge for a nightcap. After a little bit, Paul excused himself for bed and Dawn and I sat together a while longer. Paul and I had clicked instantly, even before we met in person. I wanted that same type of connection with Dawn, but we were getting to know each other just a little bit at a time.

There were no great revelations made that evening, but we enjoyed ourselves and it was a successful first meeting. We met for breakfast the next morning in the hotel and decided to get together again in a few months, then said our goodbyes in the lobby. On my ride home to the Bronx I thought about our evening and I was happy. I was glad I had listened to my gut and followed that push to look for my father. He was gone, but I could get to know more about him through Dawn and Paul. I had gained a brother and a sister in the process.

After that first meeting, we kept in touch by text or phone. Over the holidays we texted holiday greetings to each other. Paul texted more often in the beginning and we did the same in 2012. We had our own lives, families and jobs and didn't have so much time to get together. In June of 2012 Dawn and I met at Foxwoods casino, but Paul wasn't able to join us. I made the reservation and asked Dawn if I should book two rooms, or would she be willing to share one room. I looked forward to an opportunity to build our relationship. Dawn suggested one room, and that we visit the spa for massages.

We met in the lobby of the hotel and then checked into our room. We were more relaxed than our first meeting and things went well. We had dinner, played slots, and saw a comedy show. We were getting to know each other in tiny increments, but still a bit cautious. At one point we were talking about our parents and I said something about her mother. I could see her back go up at my remark and realized how protective she was. I'd have to be more careful with how I said things in the future. As I thought about it, I knew I had reacted the same way when Paul used the word *vindicated*.

Around the time I found Paul I was under a lot of stress at work and went to see a therapist. We talked about my childhood, family, and all the things that you would expect a therapist to want to discuss. She was particularly interested in my relationship or lack thereof with my father and was following my progress with Paul. During the time when he went to Boston to talk to his mother and sister, my therapist and I discussed how Carol might react and agreed that it wouldn't be well. I considered that Carol might know only what my father had claimed; that I wasn't his. This led to discussion of what role she may have played in keeping my father and I apart, if any. At the time I couldn't understand why she would care if he wanted to be in touch with me. My therapist patiently explained to me that, if this was the case, she might see me as a threat to her own family. I had no idea what their marriage was like, didn't know if they were happy, didn't know anything about them at all. As I thought more about it I realized that my therapist could be right.

Part of me blamed Carol for keeping me a secret. In 2005 when I was diagnosed with anal cancer, Aunt Barbara called Carol to find out if there was any family history. It isn't hereditary, but we didn't know that at the time. Carol asked Barbara how she'd found her. Barbara explained she'd called her old number and spoken to Paul. Carol immediately asked her if she'd mentioned anything about me to Paul. Barbara assured her that she hadn't. She said Carol calmed down at the response and told her that there was no family history as far as she knew. Carol asked her to tell my mother that she was sorry to hear I was sick.

My mother told me that she wasn't surprised when Aunt Barbara shared Carol's sympathy with her. I must have looked confused because she looked at me and said "Carol is a good person, Diane. We were friends once."

I realized that there was more to the relationships between my mother, my father and Carol than I understood and that I shouldn't place blame on any one of them.

It was July of 2013 before I saw Paul and Dawn in person again. We had of course spoken on the telephone occasionally, and texted in between. We decided to meet in New Jersey to celebrate Paul's 50th birthday. He wanted to go fishing on one of the charter boats that went out from Sandy Hook, and we agreed to go. Dawn and I met at the hotel Friday afternoon and then met Paul in a local pub for dinner and drinks. The place was crowded and there was a band set up to start playing. We moved to the bar after we ate and played a couple of games of pool. As Paul seemed to know a large number of people in the place I figured it was a regular hangout for them. Some guy clumsily bumped into us, and didn't bother to apologize. Paul yelled over to him "Hey buddy, you just knocked into us; it's customary to say to you're sorry when that happens."

The guy ignored him. Paul didn't say anything else. A little while later when Paul was at the pool table, something happened with the same guy and an argument started. They were chest to chest yelling and I could see that Paul was furious. He told the guy to meet him outside and they could settle it there, then immediately turned and went outside. Dawn and I followed after him, both hoping that it wouldn't escalate any further. The guy looked like he wasn't sure he should follow, but decided he had to at that point since they'd attracted the attention of most of the bar. Outside Dawn was trying to talk Paul down while I stood there not knowing what to do. The guy came out but it was apparent that he didn't want to take it to the next level. He apologized and then it was over. We left shortly after with plans to meet at the waterfront the next day.

We met at Paul's apartment instead. He texted Dawn in the morning that we wouldn't make the charter he wanted to do, so we could sleep a bit later. We went in Paul's truck to the docks, to see if we could pick up a different boat going out, but ended up not going fishing that day. Instead we walked around looking at all the boats, and went into a restaurant right on the waterfront for lunch. I have always had a love for the ocean and being near the water soothes me. We sat outside on the deck, enjoying the weather and looking at the water. Paul said he was just as happy to spend the time relaxing with his sisters and enjoying the view. We sat there for a few hours, talking and having a couple of beers during the course of the day. We had the waitress take a couple of photos of us and really enjoyed the time we spent together.

We talked about where and when we should meet again and thought we might try to meet towards the end of the summer. Dawn's birthday was August 7 and mine was August 22. All three of us were Leos, with our birthdays falling between July 22 and August 22. We talked about that; was this a coincidence? We decided that our dad must have been particularly frisky in the fall. As it turns out, we didn't meet again that summer and it was the last time the three of us enjoyed each other's company.

ELEVEN

HERE AND GONE

On the afternoon of January 2, 2014, I was sitting on my sofa watching television. It had been a rainy New Year's Day as a nor'easter had interrupted the holiday with heavy winds and rain. The telephone rang, and since my caller ID was visible on the television at that time, I knew Dawn was calling My stomach clenched; it was unusual for her to call unexpectedly. I answered saying "Hey you! How're you doing?" I knew something was wrong and Dawn's voice confirmed it for me.

"Well, I have some bad news. I'm sorry but I thought you should know…Paul's had an accident."

On full alert now, I couldn't help but interrupt her. "How bad?"

"He's in the ICU right now, and it's touch and go" she replied.

"Oh my God, what happened?" I exclaimed.

"It seems he fell off of a roof" Dawn answered . "I don't have all the details, but mom and I are at the hospital and it's not looking good."

Paul had been working for a company installing satellite dishes at the time. I sat there stunned. "Ok, I want to come. Is it ok if I come to the hospital? I can't believe this is happening..."

Dawn took a breath before she answered. "Yes, I think you should be here too, if you want to come."

She gave me the information for the hospital and we disconnected. My body had kicked into crisis mode and I got on the internet and booked a hotel room not far from the hospital. I notified work that I had a family emergency and might be out for a day or two. I threw some clothing into a bag and let my kids know that I was going to be in New Jersey at least overnight, and told them about Paul. They were all old enough to be left on their own at this time. My boyfriend of many years was living with me at the time, and said he would come with me. We got into his truck, were on the road, and at the hospital just after dark.

The hospital was quiet already, with the lobby lights dimmed. The security guard gave us directions to the ICU waiting room. There were several people there when we arrived. Dawn must have been in with Paul because I didn't see her, but a petite woman with short blonde hair and a vape in her hand looked up as we entered the room.

"Diane?" she asked.

I realized this must be Carol, so I nodded and said "Carol?"

She nodded in return, and turned to a rather large man sitting nearby and she asked him to go get Dawn. Before he left he came over and put his hand out to me.

"I'm Paul, Dawn's husband."

"Glad to meet you." I shook his hand and introduced Glenn as my boyfriend and they shook hands as well. Carol had gotten up and come over towards us, and as I turned toward her she put her arms out for a hug.

"Sorry to meet you like this" she said as we hugged.

I couldn't respond, but introduced Glenn to her as well. They also hugged. I was unsuccessfully fighting back tears as we sat across from each other. Carol looked exhausted and worn out but it was obvious that she was an attractive woman. I could see Dawn in her face and thought that she was similar in appearance to my own mother. Some of the other people in the room started introducing themselves also. A woman who looked to be my age or slightly younger shook my hand and said she was Lisa, Dawn's best friend. There were several other friends of Dawn and Paul in the room as well. We said hello to each of them and then waited for Dawn. She came into the room a moment later, looking quite drawn. We hugged each other, and I introduced Glenn. She asked if I wanted to go in to see Paul.

On the way to Paul's bed, which was down the hallway and to the left, Dawn explained that he had been working on a satellite dish on the roof of a home, in spite of the rainy weather and had fallen off the roof. The owner found him but didn't know how long he'd been laying there. He'd broken his neck as well as more other bones than I can remember and was on a ventilator to help him breathe. The doctors said he was in bad shape. He had been in surgery for some time, and that they had induced a coma to allow his body time to heal. If he lived through the next 48 hours, he might survive but would be paralyzed at least from the waist down. I was feeling rather numb by the time we got into his actual room. The severity of his injuries had stunned me. There was a woman in the room, who left as we entered. I saw Paul in the bed but couldn't believe it was him. His head was bandaged and his face was swollen and bruised. Every other part of his body was wrapped in bandages and casts, etc. Glenn had come with us, and stood behind Dawn and myself at Paul's bedside. Dawn and I had clasped hands at some point before entering the room, and we just stood there, looking at Paul. We were both crying silently. Dawn said they'd told her that we should talk to him, that he might still hear us.

She spoke to Paul: "Diane is here, Paul."

Dawn said she was going to leave the room and come back in a few minutes. Glenn left with her, and I was alone with Paul. I very gently rubbed the hand which wasn't bandaged like the rest of him. I was extremely gentle since I wasn't sure if the hand was injured, though it didn't appear to be.

"Hello Paul" I started. " I don't know if you can hear me but I want to tell you something. You've given me the greatest gift by accepting me as your sister. I don't know how to explain it but it's meant so much to me. I love you, brother. You need to get better. I can't lose you, we have so many years to catch up on. You were supposed to take me fishing, remember?"

When Dawn finally came back into the room she stood next to me.

"You ok?" she asked.

"Not really," I answered.

We held on to each other tightly for a minute and Dawn suggested we go back outside for a while so her Mom could come back in. We walked out together and as we neared the waiting room, the woman who'd been in the room when I'd first entered was standing in the hallway. She was a little taller than me, heavier set and was quite pretty; she had an Irish look about her.

"This is Linda, Paul's wife." Dawn said. We hugged for a moment.

"Paul was very excited about you," Linda said. "He told me all about how you met."

I smiled, as I realized that she was offering me some comfort in the only way she could. We went back into the waiting room and sat down. Carol got up and went down the hall. We continued that way for hours, someone went in for a while, then came out so someone else could go in. None of us knew what we were waiting for, but we all wanted to be near Paul.

At one point Carol looked over at me.

"What a shame," she said. "You just found him... to lose him so quickly" shaking her head.

My eyes filled with tears, and hers did also. I was touched by her kindness and concern for me while it was her son on the brink of death.

"We haven't lost him yet," I murmured. She nodded, but she had an air of defeat around her.

Eventually we left the hospital, checked in at the hotel and did it all over again the next day. Paul was holding his own and was doing as well as could be expected. The day passed slowly with a new set of friends and family coming in to lend support to Carol and Dawn. As the morning merged into afternoon and then evening, we were tired and hungry and needed a break. Dawn said she wanted to get her mother out for a while, and get dinner. I suggested that we go together, if that was all right. They picked a nearby restaurant and we departed and met up there. There were six of us; Dawn, Carol, Carol's cousin and an old friend of theirs, Glenn and myself. It was a casual place but it was busy and we ordered drinks to get started. Everyone relaxed into casual conversation. Carol's cousin and friend asked me polite questions about my children and my work.

When Glenn and I had arrived at the hospital that morning they were there with Carol already. Introductions had been made and I knew that both of them had already heard all about me by the looks on their faces when my name was mentioned. They were nice enough people and as we ordered our food and ate, the conversation included much humor and laughter.

I was struck by the realization that these people were no different from the people around me in my own life. My mother's friends and cousins could have been substituted for these women and the feeling at the table and the laughter would have been the same. I had romanticized my father so much as a little girl, that for some reason I believed that his family and friends would be somehow better than those I had grown up with. That sounds ridiculous to me now, but it is the truth. Recognizing that they were no different was a step in the right direction in my personal healing.

When we'd finished eating Glenn paid the check over the protests of all present. He said it wasn't often that he'd had an opportunity to sit at a table with so many beautiful ladies, and that it was his pleasure to get the check. One of the ladies turned to me and asked me if he was rich. I thought for a second and replied that yes, he was, in many ways. They chuckled at that and then we all departed. The ladies were going home but Glenn and I were staying the night, so we went back to the hospital. We planned to head home in the morning as we had work to get back to.

I wanted to say goodbye to Paul and let him know that I would be thinking about him. He had passed the critical point and was still with us, but he wasn't completely out of the woods yet. Dawn had notified her job that she was going to be out for an extended period and she and Carol would be staying on for the time being.

I went in and sat with Paul for a few minutes and tried to process all that I was feeling. While Paul and I had clicked immediately, and a bond was formed between us, I recognized that the emotions I was feeling would be so much more intense if it were my brother Tommy I was sitting with at the moment. The blood relation would be exactly the same: half-brother with one shared parent, my mother for Tommy, and father for Paul. The difference was that one I'd grown up with and the other I'd only just met, relatively speaking.

I recognized that this was brutal for Dawn. She had included me as family when she called me about Paul, and had acknowledged my right to be there at the hospital with them and I was grateful. However, I knew that our suffering was different. As I acknowledged these thoughts, my empathy for her grew and I felt more connected to her than I had previously. When we were ready to leave, I squeezed her just a little tighter.

Over the next few weeks we kept in touch via text messages and phone calls. Paul was off the ventilator and they had allowed him to emerge from the coma. He was out of ICU and was in stable condition. He was in pain, and trying to deal emotionally with the trauma of realizing that he would never walk again. He had use of his arms and could move his head which was fantastic to those of us who loved him, but he wasn't seeing it that way at the moment.

Paul had been given his phone and could text but he wasn't really in the mood for it. Dawn told me that he was being moved to a rehab facility. She had researched and found one of the best in the country and arranged for him to go there. It was in New Jersey so it would be convenient for Linda and little Paul to see him. Dawn was working on finding a wheelchair and a place that could accommodate him after rehab. I think she wanted Paul to come up to Boston and be in a facility near her home, but Paul wasn't having that. Dawn had taken over many of the responsibilities for managing his care. She was exhausted, frustrated, sad and overwhelmed.

Paul was making it clear that he wished he had died and had no desire to live in his current condition. He had also been off of his medication and his bipolar disorder was in full swing. His depression was intense and he was so full of anger that he scared most people away. The hospital was trying to get all of his medications to balance; he had been on so many painkillers and other medications that this was not an easy fix. I texted and got minimal responses from him.

"Hello honey, I'm not really in the mood to talk. I don't understand why my family didn't just let me die. I hate this fucking place."

His anger was focused on his mother and sister; he blamed them for allowing the hospital to put him on a ventilator, and for all of it. I asked if I could come see him, but he said he really wasn't good company and wasn't in the mood for visitors.

I did get to see him once while he was in the rehabilitation hospital. I brought him a happy face balloon, to try to cheer him up. Paul had a tattoo on his arm of a happy face in honor of our father. Dad had loved to draw happy faces when he wrote a note, and always made a happy face egg at Easter. Paul looked at the balloon as I walked into his room and said it was cute. I met my nephew Paul that day. Young Paul was about fifteen years old at the time, and pretty tall for his age. He was a good looking young man. He was there with his mom and Bill, Paul's friend who was married to Lisa, Dawn's friend. I'd met them briefly at the hospital when Paul was in the ICU. Paul introduced me to his son.

"Hey Paulie, I want you to say hello to your Aunt Diane. You remember that I told you about her?" Young Paul looked at me, said "Hi," and asked "My aunt?"

"Yes, she's your aunt." Paul said gently to his son. However, he couldn't maintain that demeanor for very long. I sat down and asked him how he was doing, which was probably a mistake. He looked me in the eye and told me that he was miserable.

"I hate this fucking place. It's a fucking prison." As he said this his voice went up and his agitation increased.

Bill got up. "Come on, Paulie. Let's go for a walk; see what they have for snacks around here."

Young Paul got up and went with him immediately and I could see that he was familiar and comfortable with Bill. Paul ranted on about the nurses, the food, even the other patients.

"I'm only here because my family is selfish. They didn't think about what I would want."

He truly was miserable, and I was sorry I'd asked him. He had worked himself up into a bit of a frenzy, and there was nothing I could do to help. Linda had obviously seen this before, and she didn't react to it at all, other than to calmly tell him to calm down. I felt responsible for this outburst and excused myself to use the ladies room. I don't know what she may have said to him while I was gone, but he was strangely calmer when I came back to the room.

He looked at me and said "I told you that I wasn't very good company." I acknowledged his statement with a nod.

He was eventually released from the rehab facility. That was a terrible year for him; he developed a bed sore that became a crater in his bottom. It got infected with MRSA and he needed surgery on it. His temperament didn't improve very much, as I realized from his texts. He would occasionally post updates on Facebook which I looked forward to reading. Paul had a great sense of humor and it came through in his posts. For example, one day he wrote: "Fun fact: it is impossible to sweat below the point at which the spine was severed. I will never have sweaty balls again." Here's another:

"My life is a 'K' turn, and other amusing insights from the chair. I am thinking that should be the title of the book everyone wants me to write. Like unplanned wheelies r no fun (crunched my head, again). There is no way to sit for 12 hrs a day and not get pressure wounds on your ass. Dignity is overrated. Rugs r bad, hard wood is good. Watch your step, one patch of ice can ruin your whole day. Life in a wheelchair sucks. I'll think of more. Hope everyone out there is well."

He threatened to kill himself when he was talking to his mother on the telephone. She called the police and they came to his apartment and took him back to the hospital and put him on a psychiatric watch. At some point, they did get his meds under control, and a calmer Paul posted this on Facebook:

"OK, here's what happened... the infectious disease doc put me on an antibiotic that conflicted with my antidepressants. So I stopped taking the psychotropic drugs and by the end of the week I wanted to kill myself. I scared my mother and she called the Sayreville cops to come get me. They took me to the hospital where I was held captive for three days. Back on my meds now, feeling better. There's a reason I take them. Thanks all."

Paul died on May 30, 2015. My first thought was that he'd killed himself, but the autopsy revealed that he'd had a blood clot to his lung. Dawn had the unfortunate duty of letting me know and making the arrangements for his funeral. It was to be held in Oldbridge, New Jersey where they had lived when the family first moved from the Bronx. I felt oddly detached from my emotions when Dawn called and gave me the news. She held herself together but I could tell by her voice that she was near the breaking point. When we hung up, I sat on the sofa, trying to process the fact that Paul was gone.

I had only known him for four years and we'd been together in person only twice, but he had earned a special place in my heart just the same. I made a hotel reservation near the funeral home and let work know that I would be out. When I told my kids they were supportive and protective of me. My oldest son Anthony said that he was sorry that he would never get to meet his uncle and wanted to come with me to the services. Danny and Lauren echoed the same sentiments. Later, when I was alone in bed I thought about how Dawn must be feeling. My heart was heavy at losing Paul, but I understood how hers must be broken. When I thought how Carol must be feeling, it was more than I could bear and I turned my thoughts away quickly.

We found the funeral home without too much trouble and the three of us went in. Dawn spotted us and came over as we signed the guest book and entered. We hugged and I introduced her to my kids Anthony, Danny and Lauren.

"This is your Aunt Dawn," They each hugged her and said they were sorry for her loss. Linda was nearby with young Paul and I introduced them to her as well. She told young Paul that he should remember me from the hospital, as Aunt Diane, and that these were his cousins.

"My cousins?" he repeated, questioning this new information.

"Yes, that's right" Linda responded. Much like his father, he seemed pleased at the thought of finding new family members so late in the game.

Anthony shook his hand, and said "I'm happy to meet you, cousin Paul, but I'm very sorry for your loss."

I noticed several people looking over at us and we stood there, and suspected that they knew who we were already. We made our way to Carol, and I told her how sorry I was and hugged her. She said she was sorry for me too, and the introductions began again. She was very sweet to my kids as they expressed their condolences. As we moved to let others approach Carol, I said I needed to find the ladies room. The detachment I felt took that moment to abandon me, and I could not hide my tears.

When I emerged from the ladies room, my kids were waiting for me. Anthony wrapped me in his arms and held me for a moment, and I felt protected and proud at the same time. When my grandmother had passed in 2002, Anthony was by my side at her wake, and at the cemetery when she was buried. He had put his arm around me as we stood there, and I knew he was sad to lose his great-grandmother, but he was there to support me. Danny hugged me as Anthony let go and I realized how glad I was to have them there with me.

Dawn came over to where we were standing and locked eyes with me.

"Are you ok?" she asked.

I nodded and said I was fine, and we made our way back into the room. She called her sons, Kevin and Danny, over and introduced them to me and my kids. They said hello politely and quickly moved back to where they had been standing. As Dawn left to greet others who were arriving, Lauren turned to me.

"Ma, Dawn looks just like you."

I scoffed at that; "No, she looks more like her mother, don't you think?"

The boys agreed with Lauren but I didn't see it at all.

"She has the same mannerisms" Anthony added. They were fascinated by what they saw as the similarities between the two of us.

Bill came over to say hello. He told me that he had worked for my father for a while when he was a teen, and that he had looked up to and respected him. I introduced him to my kids, telling them that he had known their grandfather.

Lauren looked excited and said "Really? You knew Grandpa? How did you know him?"

The way she asked told me that she thought I meant Sal's father Tony, the grandfather she knew and loved who had passed a few years earlier.

"No, Lauren, I mean my father who was also your grandfather."

"Oh." she said, looking more disappointed than embarrassed.

Her brothers smirked and said hello to Bill. After that everyone was asked to take a seat and Dawn got up to speak. She talked about growing up with Paul as her older brother. She described his protectiveness as well as the fights they were famous for. She held her tears back but I heard them in her voice several times. She then invited any others who wanted to speak about Paul to come to the front and do so. Several of his friends got up to speak, one after the other. As each described him, I could feel his presence there in the room with us.

One of my kids asked if I was going to speak but I shook my head no. I'd thought about it carefully before I'd left home and even worried about how I'd introduce myself to those gathered.

In the end I decided against speaking because I didn't think I'd earned the right after knowing him for such a short time. I also worried that some in the group would resent me. I let those fears determine my actions, as I had let other fears control me in the past.

After the service, everyone was invited to a nearby restaurant for lunch. Dawn checked in with me to make sure that we would be joining them. I said we would. When we entered the place we were told to sit anywhere, and there was a small table for four people on the side of the room. I chose that table and we sat. Once again, I was grateful to have my kids with me. If I were alone, I might not have come. I would have felt too self-conscious sitting by myself. We ordered a drink and talked about the service. The boys were teasing Lauren about thinking Bill had known their paternal grandfather. She was laughing about it as well.

Danny saw Bill enter the room and said "Hey look there's Grandpa Bill," and we all chuckled.

Whenever the subject of Paul or Dawn comes up till this day, one of them will remember the *Grandpa Bill* story. After a little while Carol came over to the table. She said how nice it was that the kids had come and that she wished she had met us under happier circumstances. She then said that she would love for us all to get together at another time. She stood with her hand on Anthony's shoulder as she spoke to us. We all agreed that it would be great if we could, and Carol moved away.

I was touched that she had made sure to come over to us, and that she was so gracious with my children. A short while later, there was a commotion at another table where an older woman had slumped over in her chair and people were jumping up to go to her. Someone yelled to call an ambulance, and they stood over her. It was Linda's mother, and Linda was with her trying to revive her. They got there very quickly, and took the woman out and to the hospital. We were silent as all of this occurred. I felt sorry for Linda, who just lost her husband (or ex-husband really) and now faced the threat of losing her mother. Her mother did pass that day, unfortunately. Young Paul had lost his father and maternal grandmother in the span of a couple of days.

In the year after Paul passed my thoughts kept returning to the meditation I had done on the bus in which I'd felt my grandmother was with me. I started thinking about consulting a medium in order to speak to my father and Paul. My daughter had talked about seeing a medium with her father and aunt after their parents had passed. They had gone more than once, and she said that the information they received from the medium had been very accurate. He was located on Long Island, and it was a bit of a trip to see him. I told her that I would like to make an appointment and she said she would get the information. Then she told me that she had heard of another medium who was located much closer to where we lived, and she had been thinking about scheduling an appointment with this lady.

Lauren booked an appointment for the both of us and offered it to me as my birthday gift that year. However, the medium had a long waiting list and we had to wait a few weeks before we could see her. In the meantime, I had been transferred to the Bronx office to work as a grievance specialist. I kept in touch with Dawn, but it was usually every couple of months when one of us would send a text message or call. Dawn was busy with Carol who was ill. She was diagnosed with cancer of the gallbladder and had begun treatment. All of Dawn's energy was focused on Carol and getting her well. She was trying to remain positive and hoping that the treatments would work. She took a few weeks off at one point and traveled to California with her mother. They rented a car and drove up the coast, exploring and visiting friends and family as they went. We talked when they got back, and she seemed pretty upbeat. They'd had a good time and many laughs.

Dawn had been through the wringer after she split from her husband and sold her house and moved further north to a beautiful little coastal town near the border of New Hampshire. Carol was initially responding to the treatments, but the cancer had progressed. Dawn set her up in the den on the main floor of the house so Carol wouldn't have to go up and down stairs.

Dawn and I spoke occasionally and I wondered how she was managing with all she was going through. In the spring of 2016 I sent two baskets of daisies to Dawn's new address for Mother's Day. Dawn called to thank me and said her mother was thrilled because she loved daisies.

Carol and Dawn had been talking about final arrangements, and Carol wanted a party to visit with all her friends and family while she was still alive. When Dawn invited me, I wasn't sure if Carol approved. Dawn assured me that Carol would like me to attend, and Dawn wanted me there as well.

Dawn sent out invitations to *The Party of a Lifetime,* and asked people to share their favorite stories about Carol. It was upbeat and positive and I thought it was a fabulous idea. The party was scheduled for late June. I waited too long to find a hotel room nearby and found one twenty minutes away. It was a four hour drive from my house, and I drove up the morning of the party to check into the hotel. I was a little anxious about being there since Dawn would be busy and I didn't know anyone else.

I knew I would be self-conscious, but I was going anyway. I stopped and bought some wine and a cheese plate so I wouldn't be empty-handed. I rang the doorbell and a woman I didn't know greeted me. She invited me in and introduced herself as Liz, Dawn's friend. I told her that I was Diane, Dawn's new sister. She laughed and asked if I wanted a drink. She offered to take the food and wine I'd brought out to the tables in the yard. Dawn had a large tent, tables and chairs set up in the backyard. As I came out the back door Dawn came over and gave me a hug. She asked how the ride was, and if I'd had any trouble finding the house. She walked me over the coolers where the beer was and I chose something. She said she would be running around, but I should make myself comfortable, and she went to greet someone else who had just arrived.

I recognized a few people from the hospital when Paul was in ICU, and I walked over and said hello to a few that were standing nearby. They were all nice enough, and I kind of just hung out near them for a while. There were several women who were bringing food from upstairs and generally helping out. Dawn has a great circle of friends who all pitched in that day. Carol was seated in the tent, and I went to say hello, kissing her on the cheek. She smiled and said she was glad I could come. She had a group gathered near her, and I recognized one of the ladies who had joined us for dinner when Paul was in the hospital. She smiled and nodded in greeting and I did the same. I moved away so they could go back to whatever they had been talking about. I wasn't as uncomfortable as I thought I'd be and the time went quickly.

Dawn had food catered from a restaurant nearby, and people grabbed plates and sat to eat. Dawn announced that she wanted to make a toast, and started by thanking everyone for coming. She told a funny story about her mom, and everyone laughed. She made a toast, and then invited anyone who wanted to share a story to do so. There were a few stories, all very funny. It was a beautiful party and everyone enjoyed it, especially Carol. It was obvious that she was frail, and she had to be assisted into the house to use the bathroom a few times. I could see the decline in her health from when I'd seen her last. When she took a break from her hostess duties, Dawn came over and we sat a few minutes. She said that Carol had not been doing well, and had been in a great deal of pain, and out of it from the medication a good deal of the time. She was amazed at how she'd rallied for this party, and was concerned that it might be exhausting her. I recognized that Dawn was an amazing person, and a good daughter. She obviously had a very close relationship with her mom and I knew she would be heartbroken to lose her. I wished I lived closer, so I could help out and so I could be there for her, and told her so. She thanked me, and said she would be ok. I wasn't so sure.

Carol passed on July 22, 2016. Dawn called to tell me, and I could tell she was holding herself together by a thread. I asked about services, but she said it wasn't necessary for me to come. I wanted to be there to support her but she didn't budge. She said I had come to the party and she and her mom had appreciated that. I didn't argue with her as I sensed that she had accepted me as her sister, and had already shared her father's memory and her brother with me. Carol belonged to her alone, and I understood that. As much as I wanted to be there to support Dawn, I respected her wishes. I still worried because she'd lost both her mother and father, as well as her brother. I silently vowed to keep in touch with her more.

About a month later in August, Glenn and I took a trip to Vermont for a few days. Glenn was a big fan of the outdoors and loved being in nature. He also rode a Harley, and spent his free time riding as much as he could. In the summer he liked to find hidden swimming holes. He would take off on the bike wearing lightweight and quick dry shorts under his clothes, and if he came upon a place to take a dip, he did. He would spend time researching on the internet to find new and beautiful places to try. He wanted to try an abandoned rock quarry in Vermont that he had read about, so that's where we headed. I asked him if he would want to stop by Dawn's for a night or two if she was available, since we would be driving past the area where she lived. He said he would love to. I called to see how she felt about it and she said she would love for us to come. I booked us a room at a bed and breakfast place near the quarry for a couple of nights, and looked forward to seeing Dawn. The rock quarry was packed when we arrived since tons of people searched the internet for hidden swimming holes. We still enjoyed it, but I wouldn't go out of my way to get back there. The owner of the B&B told us about a state park that wasn't far away with a lake 100 times better and cleaner than the quarry. She wasn't wrong; Emerald Lake is spectacular. It isn't very large, but the water is absolutely pristine and you can see all of the little rocks and pebbles on the bottom even in the very deep areas. We spent a great day floating around and exploring, and the next day we drove to Dawn's.

When we got to her house she was happy to see us. Her dog Huck was cautious around us for about a minute, and then he was all over us. We are both dog lovers and Huck was given tons of attention; back and belly rubs. We wanted to take Dawn out to dinner for a belated birthday celebration, but she'd already made a reservation at a trendy place in town for us. Dawn and Glenn fought over the check because she had a gift certificate she wanted to use, and we insisted that dinner was on us. I had picked up a handbag for her in the Coach outlet in Vermont as a gift for her birthday although we didn't normally exchange gifts. I wanted to do something special for her. After dinner we walked around the town a bit, then headed back to the house. Dawn opened a bottle of wine and shared some very old photos of my mother, then gave them to me. She'd been going through old photos with her mom and when she asked who it was Carol had matter of factly stated "Oh, that's Frances."

"Diane's mother?" Dawn asked.

Carol affirmed that it was. These were nice 5X7 photos of my mother at age seventeen and I thanked Dawn several times for giving them to me. I think we were both incredulous that her mom had kept the photos. Dawn told me that before her mom had passed, she asked her if she had any regrets about her life. Carol said she regretted not pushing my father to see me. I didn't react to Dawn's statement, and she asked me if I'd heard what she said.

"Yes, I heard you," I said.

We didn't say anything else about it. We looked at old photos of our father and Carol, and I felt Dawn was giving me a special gift that night. She also pulled out some things our father had written over the years. There was quite a collection, and I read a few pieces. Some were funny, some sad. Dawn told me that Dad suffered from cluster headaches, and would also withdraw and become quiet and sullen at times. She said he had his flaws, and was not the perfect father or husband. I accepted what she shared with me, gratefully.

A few weeks later I got a package in the mail. She had compiled our father's writing into a small book and sent it to me. Inside the front cover she had written: "For my sister Diane - I know it's not much, not nearly enough. Hope this brings more smiles than tears. With much love, Dawn."

I was touched, beyond words. She had included the poems he wrote for Carol on various Valentine's Days, filled with love and humor. But there were also story poems. As I read one, I thought about my mother. It was about an early love, and struggle in that she had been unfaithful and denied it.

He wrote about his own pride and the hypocrisy in his reaction, as he had another woman all along. It was left sort of open-ended, like there was unfinished business and "both were still caught in love's crazy whirl." It made me sad to read it. I was also struck by the honesty and vulnerability of his writing.

The last story was about a man who abandoned his daughter, then quit drinking and gambling to get her back at the request of his dead wife's spirit. The girl's mother had died in childbirth, and he blamed the little girl who was born blind.

Although it's fiction, there are glimpses of reality just below the surface. As I read it, I knew he had many regrets, and that not claiming me was one of them. I called Dawn to thank her, and told it that it was the best gift I'd ever received in my life, and it truly was.

TWELVE
HONEY: MY FATHER'S SHORT STORY

I was trying to cure a hangover with a walk through Central Park.

It's peaceful in the morning, terrifying after dark.

The smell of the grass and the fresh air started to clear my head.

Walking towards me was a stranger with the look of the living dead.

His face was scarred and battered, his nose was broken flat.

His clothes were worn and mended, he wore a grimy hat.

His feet were barely covered; his nails were broken and black.

His worldly goods were stored in a dirty canvas sack.

He walked with a peculiar shuffle and his head bobbed from side to side.

There was a twitch in his left shoulder as his hand hung by his side.

A derelict, a bum he would seem, but his eyes were clear and his battered face with its fixed little grin was strangely calm and serene.

There was something about him that touched me — that shuffling hulk dressed in trash.

So I called him and offered him aid in the shape of five dollars cash.

His voice when he spoke was hardly a croak and he stumbled on most of the words.

"No thank you, young man, I am no beggar, though your offer is most kind.

Give your money where it's needed; give it to the blind."

Then he tipped his hat and tried to smile and started to walk away.

I begged him to stop and sit with me, to pass the time of day.

Tell me your story, I pleaded.

You are a most intriguing man.

Tell me how you came to this state, I'll try to understand.

He stared in my eyes for a moment looking for something there.

He seemed to see right through me; my heart beat fast with fear.

Then he nodded his head slightly as his eyes broke their hold.

We sat on a bench together and this is the story he told.

I was a prize fighter in my youth sir, as you can plainly see, a heavyweight contender, they were going to make a champ of me. I was up among the good ones, right at the top of the pile. And then I fell in love, with some freckles, a pug nose and a smile.

He paused for a moment, raising his head to the sky, then his shoulder sagged and he started again with a sigh.

Oh, my honey, how I loved her, I begged her to be my wife and she loved me, but too much to see me fight. So I did a good thing and quit the ring, bought a house and a bar with my money. I'd done all of this for a smile and a kiss and a freckled face wife I called Honey.

How clear he spoke when he said her name and look on his face was hardly the same.

Oh Lord, we were happy! We were so much in love, I thought nothing could add to my joy.

But I really went wild when I got her with child and of course I hoped for a boy.

She carried with pride as the baby inside grew till I thought Honey would burst.

She must've known pain but she would never complain, no tears, just smiles for my honey.

Then it last came the day and still she was gay, her smile as always was sunny.

But she died giving birth to a fair little girl and for her I named the girl Honey.

I went mad in my grief and I had the belief that the little girl killed my dear wife.

Oh God I went wild! I hated that child!

That blonde stranger who murdered my Honey.

I wanted to die and I gave it a try but my courage gave out in the end.

I took a drink out of shame, but it came out the same, liquor is slower but surer my friend.

I put the child in a home and went out alone, to kill sorrow with rum for a weapon.

My plan was to drink till I just couldn't think, to soak myself till I was numb.

I drank till I stunk, and was falling down drunk. No use, my plan was just dumb.

For sober or reeling, the vision and feeling of Honey was with me I swear.

I could see her so plain and to add to my pain, her smile was replaced by a tear.

Well I stayed with the grog, still seeking a fog that would blot out all memories and hurt.

Then I found myself begging for a mouth full of wine. I became the worst kind of dirt.

Then came a brawl, police, court and all, naturally I ended in jail.

NUDGED BY SPIRIT

A bum with no soul, assigned to a hole with others who had visions to haunt them.

Here lived the lame and were we to blame?

Poor cripples that fate had done wrong.

There was a stench in that cell, a queer sort of smell, it was self-pity and by God it could choke you.

And that's where I stayed, without any aid, no crutch to help win the fight.

And often I think that without any drink, why I didn't go mad in the night.

Oh, night time was hell in that tight little cell,

the sobs, the crying, the moans, the half stifled screams,

from these twisted gray men, who suffered through wineless dreams.

Ninety days for my crime, ninety days was my fine, ninety days with the dregs of the earth.

How I loathed them, the scum. But before I was done,

I woke up screaming along with the rest.

I was back on the street with the curb at my feet, just one drink away from the gutter.

Then a man came my way and helped plan my day with an offer to earn a fiver.

The man had three trucks and offered the bucks to unload them with the help of the driver.

DIANE FRANCES

We finished our chore; I got five and one more, the extra for working so hard.

Six bucks I had earned with a body that burned and muscles that were covered with lard.

My hands were raw and my back was sore,

My legs, Lord, how they ached me.

But what was the worst was the terrible thirst,

That had been waiting for 90 long days.

Six bucks was all mine, six bucks to buy wine,

to feed the crawling inside and when it was done,

I'd be the one to crawl in a bottle to hide.

Sure the outlook is bleak for a man who is weak, a wino that gave up the fight.

Then I glanced at myself in a window glass and swung out enraged at the sight.

The glass stayed intact but I drew back a hand that was broken and bleeding.

Then I looked up again, seen a woman and child, it was Honey and her blue eyes were pleading.

Well it stopped me cold and cleared my head; tingles went up my spine.

She seemed to say, "the babe is yours and I should claim what was mine."

She was so alive, it was all so real, that I reached out to touch her but Honey was gone, there was only the glass to feel.

And there I froze in that impossible pose, with my hand stretched out to my wife.

And that was the instant that made up my mind and altered the course of my life.

The message was plain, it was clearly shown,

TAKE BACK OUR CHILD

TAKE CARE OF YOUR OWN!

It was odd jobs at first till I conquered the thirst,

and the shaking went out of my hands.

I met an old friend who had seen me box,

and he got me a steady job down on the docks.

The work was hard but the money was good,

there were men there like me so I knew where I stood.

I started saving and my money soon grew.

I'd have plenty for what I must do.

Giving up children is easy enough,

getting them back though, that's when it's tough.

I worked all the hours the job would permit,

and I never got tired for my body was fit.

My muscles had hardened and my wind grew long,

I was still in my prime and terribly strong.

But along with my heath came desire.

DIANE FRANCES

So I turned to the gym to help douse the fire.

For ten or twelve hours I worked like a mule,

Then to the gym, I'd train like a fool.

Running and jumping and punching the bag,

Boxing my shadow till the body would sag.

I'd keep this up for many an hour,

Then home for an icy cold shower.

Then on my knees for a private prayer

And desire would vanish if in truth it was there.

And this was my life day after day,

Working and training and saving my pay.

Going along at a steady grind,

month after month with one thought in mind.

To get back my child, to give her the best,

to love and keep her and let my wife rest.

Oh yes! Honey was there, at night in my dreams she eased all my fears.

And in the daytime when my spirits fell,

urging me on, wishing me well.

And every night as I ended my prayer,

I'd know peace for Honey was there.

The day I left the lawyer I hired, she was smiling so gay, but Lord she looked tired.

Now he stopped and seemed surprised to find me by his side.

I hadn't stirred since he began; I couldn't if I tried.

He wove a spell that trapped him and also captured me.

Then he said, embarrassed,

"Forgive me, I'm boring you I'm sure.

I'll say goodbye and save you from hearing anymore."

Then he stood and took his sack and made like he would go.

The thought of his leaving shook me; it hit me like a blow.

"Please sir," I pleaded, you can't, you mustn't leave me so.

I have to hear it all, the end. Please, I really want to know."

And he seeing my panic agreed, much to my relief.

"I'll tell you all, young fellow, and try to make it brief."

My heart was pounding, fit to break and my knees had turned to water.

I walked into a room of two year olds, twenty of them running free.

And I knew at once which one she was and I knew she belonged to me.

Her mother's hair, blonde like gold, milk skin touched with rose, her mother's smile, her mothers nose.

And big blue eyes that shone so bright,

This was my Honey, it was her all right.

I ran to her and fell on my knees,

"My baby, I'm here, forgive me please."

Then the words that struck me dumb

"Oh Daddy, I knew it, the pretty angel said that you would come." Then a little shyly, in a voice like a summer breeze,

Softly she said, "Oh Daddy, hold me please."

And hold her I did till I thought she'd smother,

But she didn't complain, how so like her mother.

Such a cheerful little tyke, she didn't seem to mind

that I had left her all alone and God had left her blind.

For the big blue eyes that shine so bright,

Had shown with love but not with sight.

And once more Honey came to me, with wings so she could fly,

She came to say God loves me, she came to say goodbye.

And no more did I see her, not once till this very day,

I never heard her voice again, not even when I'd pray.

We had a year together, the happiest one of my life,

I never knew such joy before, not even with my wife.

We would walk together and I would be her eyes,

I'd tell her what a bird was and how gracefully one flies.

I'd tell her of the sunsets, of how green the grass could be,

I'd tell her of all the wonderful things that she would never see.

Her little hands would touch things, a stone, a leaf, a tree,

And she would say "Oh daddy, it's nice and so are we."

Once she touched a flower and a smile came to her face,

"Let's come here again, Daddy, it's pretty in this place."

Nights I read her stories, as she curled up in my lap,

'till, sleepily she'd say to me, "I think I'll take a nap."

Then one last kiss, a children's prayer and we would say good night.

My poor little babe of darkness, would she never know the light?

Then one day my child fell ill,

and ran a high fever, as children will.

The doctor said she'd be alright,

and told me of a surgeon who could perhaps restore her sight.

I shouldn't get my hopes up, there were tests they'd have to make,

at best it would be a gamble, and one I'd have to take.

DIANE FRANCES

The tests they took were endless and painful for my Honey.

The expense was something awful and now I needed money.

I took to fighting four rounders to help offset the cost.

Then six and eight and ten and still I hadn't lost.

The tests went on: they'd soon be done.

Three more fights and still I won.

Then the day the doctor called, he said the tests were fine.

He said it would cost a fortune; he said the decision was mine.

My mind was made in an instant, I told him to make his plans.

I could get the money; I'd earn it with my hands.

Now I'd fight in earnest, a contender I would become.

Main events with some good ones, not semi's with the bums.

I told the plan to my manager; he fairly jumped with joy.

"Don't worry, you'll be a champ yet and will get the money, boy."

He arranged a good fight quickly, with a slugger just like me.

We packed the place to the rafters and I nailed my man and three.

The next fight was tougher, ah but the money was just fine.

I took a lot of pounding but dropped my man in nine.

The next two fights were sellouts against two top flight men.

I finished one and six and the other lasted ten.

The next fight was a rainbow — at the end, the pot of gold.

Boxer vs. Slugger; youth against old.

That's how the newspapers played it; that's how they put it down.

The winner of this classic bout would then fight for the crown.

Boy, you should've seen me that night, for six rounds I fought like a champ.

You know, I couldn't do anything wrong;

the left was smooth and quick and the right was knockout strong.

The kid I was fighting was a nice looking boy; you know the type — cute.

And he had this hook that came off his jab that I had to admit was a beaut.

He wasn't much of a puncher I thought;

he couldn't hit as hard as a dozen I fought.

Why, I must have had him a couple of times but I missed the big one by inches.

I worked on his body when we were in close; boy I was strong in the clinches.

He'd stay outside and bob and weave, then come on with a flurry.

In the fourth so help me I had him, I nailed him coming in.

He was off-balance and staggering, I could almost taste the win.

I straightened him out and set him up, he was ready to be put away.

But I missed it - dammit - I missed it and I still don't know how to this day.

Then in the sixth I ran out of gas, I had my chance and blew it.

My arms turned to lead and the legs went dead and the kid I was fighting knew it.

The boxing was done and the slaughter began, for nine bloody rounds I caught hell.

I just wouldn't go down and I struggled each round to come out and answer the bell.

Oh the crowd, how they loved it. They shouted and screamed,

"Knock him out!"

But I fooled them my friend, I was there at the end, only I lost more than the bout.

For that's when I started twitching, and got my shuffle and my grin.

But they gave me the money and that was the thing, so what if I didn't win.

The operation was a big success; my baby's eyes were alright.

she could come out of the darkness now; she could walk in the light.

Then I gave the good sisters all that I had: my clothes, my watch and my money.

Told them to find her a home full of love, she's easy to love my Honey.

Yeah I told the sisters to keep her now that she could see.

Cause what little girl wants a Daddy; a Daddy who looks like me.

With this, he turned his head so his tears I could not spy

And he shuffled away, and to this day, when I think of him I cry.

THIRTEEN
LIFTING THE VEIL

My daughter Lauren and I went to see the medium she'd booked as my birthday present. Her name was Terry, and she read for me first and for Lauren after. We sat in her little kitchen where she had several religious candles burning. She said a prayer before she began. "Do you have a Frank in the spirit world?" she asked.

"Frank is acknowledging an honor you gave him after he'd passed."

My mother had a long term boyfriend called Frank, who had passed on Valentine's Day in 1989. It was also the year my son Daniel was born. I had given Danny his middle name in honor of Frank. That was a pretty good way to start this reading, I thought. Next she had my grandmother who she said claimed me as a daughter. She told me my grandmother was asking when I was going to write my book.

"She says you have a book in you, and you need to get started." This struck me also, as I had done a lot of writing when I was younger, but had basically stopped as an adult.

"Do you know a Carol, no, Caroline..no wait... are you going to the Carolinas?" I was amazed, since I had recently received a "save the date" card for the wedding of my cousin Peter's son, who would be getting married on the beach in the Outer Banks of North Carolina. I said that yes, I would be going to the Carolinas and told her why.

"Well, your grandmother will be going too. She said she will be arriving in a Cadillac."

I didn't understand the Cadillac, but accepted that she would be at the wedding.

"She is saying that she had her favorites and that you knew that," she told me.

My cousin Peter was the oldest son of my Aunt Liz. My grandmother loved all of her grandchildren, but she secretly favored me, Peter and my cousin Billy. Billy was the oldest of my Aunt Claire's children. The three of us knew that we were the favorites, though I am sure she never once said so.

She then said that Nana was showing her the Blessed Mother, and touching her breast. She asked if I had any worries regarding breast cancer. I told her that my mother had breast cancer many years ago, and that I was already scheduled for a biopsy, as they'd found something on my most recent mammogram. She told me that my grandmother was assuring me that everything would be okay.

"Who is the young man who had fallen off a roof?"

"My brother," I replied, stunned.

"She wants you to know that she was with him and stayed with him when he was lying there. She was there with him for you, asking God to spare his life." I was in tears by this time and could hardly speak.

"He didn't die then, but has since," she continued. "She says he is there with her, and so is your father. She says she didn't like your father very much and that you never needed him anyway."

Terry then said that she could sense my father and gave the names Peter, or Paul. However, she didn't give me any specific evidence about my father. I was sorry not to hear something more from Dad and Paul, but she had given me evidence to believe that spirits were actually there talking to her.

Lauren was read next, and Terry brought her paternal grandparents through for her. She said Lauren had been visited by her grandmother, and that she'd sat on Lauren's bed while she was sleeping. Lauren responded that she'd dreamed exactly that, and was in tears within the first few minutes. Terry also brought through her grandfather, who Lauren always describes as her best friend. She shared evidence that he was a singer and musician and described him pretty well. Next, my grandmother came for Lauren. The medium said she knew it was the same spirit who was there for me. Lauren hardly knew Nana, who'd had dementia when Lauren was still a little girl. Nana was called G.G. by my children, a name she had picked out herself when Anthony was born.

"Lauren, You have a blue light over your head. Your great-grandmother says that when you are ready, she will assist you. You can do what I'm doing. You are a medium and can talk to spirit people."

Lauren looked at her like she was crazy. Terry asked if she had bad dreams and anxiety at night, and Lauren said she did. She explained that spirit was attracted to her because they could see that she was a medium, even if she didn't realize for herself yet. She told Lauren that Nana was saying she would work with her when she acknowledged her abilities.

Lauren was surprised by this, but my reaction was stronger. I hate to admit it, but I was jealous. I had felt drawn to something throughout my life, and hearing the medium say this to Lauren brought it all back to me. I recalled the meditation on the bus so vividly when Nana was with me. I remembered when I was in Sedona, and had woken to the sound of my Uncle Bobby's voice, telling me "something is coming." I had felt him there with me. I remembered the woman who stood next to my bed when I was still married, and feeling my dog Knuckles join me in bed after he'd already gone over the rainbow bridge.

As the medium gave this information to Lauren, I sat there wondering why she hadn't given it to me. She brought through a few other people for Lauren while I half listened. It was dawning on me, finally, that I'd had indications of my own abilities. I determined there and then to continue to explore mediumship and learn as much as I could about it.

Lauren and I talked about this experience the entire way home. She was a believer, and although she'd talked with mediums before, this was the first time someone said that she had the same ability. She was toying with the idea of exploring it further, but wasn't convinced.

On the other hand, I could think of nothing else and started looking for mediums online. I found a ton of psychic hotlines, as well as people that felt like phonies and fakes. I browsed articles and advertisements until I came across a place called the Windbridge Institute which was doing research on mediums and mediumship. I learned that the difference between a psychic and a medium is that a psychic gets information from the soul of the living (incarnate) and accesses the information from the sitter's aura which contains information about the individual. Mediums get information from the souls of the deceased (discarnate).

I found a school in East Rutherford NJ, called the Montclair Metaphysical Center, which was also known as the Montclair Psychic School. I browsed the website and looked at their class offerings, but didn't book anything right away.

I looked at other places and found Echo Bodine's website. She was offering an affordable online psychic development class and I thought it would be a good way to start so I signed up for the class. It had some pre-recorded lessons and some live sessions as well. A lot of the course was about using our intuition. Echo talked to us about listening to the still, quiet voice within ourselves. She gave us exercises to practice using our intuition and feeling the reaction in our gut when faced with choices. We did meditations designed for clearing our minds and enhancing our intuition. We were a small group and did partnered practice exercises with each other. We exchanged photos and did photo readings of people who were alive. We had to describe the person in the photo without looking at it first. After the physical description, we had to describe things they liked to do or the type of music they liked. We also sent names to each other and tried to tune in to the person, using only their name. Sometimes I was totally off in my responses, and sometimes I got a few things right.

When that class ended I signed up for *Accelerated Psychic Development* at Montclair Metaphysical. It was a one day class offered by the owner of the center, Lee VanZyl. Born in South Africa, she called herself the South African Medium. Lee had been an attorney before realizing her abilities. The day started with an introductory talk on the many ways we can use psychic abilities even if we aren't interested in doing psychic readings, then moved into a discussion of intuition and how to learn to trust it. I wrote about the experience that night, when I got home.

I went to psychic development class today at Montclair Metaphysical with Lee VanZyl. She explained terms and methods then did a chakra meditation with us. Our chakras became lotus flowers, opening and spinning clockwise, from the root to the crown. We paired up and felt the energy fields of our partners. In one exercise we put our hands over or under the hand of our partner without touching. I could feel the aura/energy of my partner as our hands got closer, well before they were close enough to touch. We also did this standing apart and coming closer. I had to ask my partner if I could enter their aura and when they said yes, I felt a gentle pull as I neared them. If they said no, it was a push as I got closer to them. I was blown away by that experience.

I could definitely feel the auras of the people I worked with and the difference when they gave me permission to enter their space or when they didn't. We did blindfolded partner readings with several different people, and several of the people I worked with said that I was correct on many of the things I felt about them. With one partner I felt a terrible loss that was connected to health issues. I also felt that he was looking for answers to the bigger questions in life, but I was overwhelmed by emotion and loss. I ended up in tears and had to stop. He said I was right, he was seeking answers, and had suffered with heath and loss.

My reaction surprised me. It took a bit of time to shake off the sadness I felt after working with him. We did several meditations during the day and one was to speak to a spirit guide. I got into the meditation easily, and felt waves of energy around me, and saw colors in my mind. I asked if I was on the right track, with my new interests and heard "Yes." I asked how I would know what to do as I moved forward, and heard "I will whisper to you." I was floored. It was very real to me, this brief conversation. I am very excited about this and so glad I took this class.

In January of 2017, six months after her mom had passed, Dawn took a leave of absence from work. She was still struggling with the cumulative loss of her parents and brother. While she initially threw herself into her work, she hadn't found any peace. She felt like she needed the time off to process and recoup. She obviously spent a lot of time thinking about life and death, and wondering what it was all about. She took a road trip with her best friend Lisa and traveled across the country and back. They had spent some time in Sedona, Arizona which is truly a magical place. While there they had massages, and Dawn opted to have a Reiki massage, with no idea what it was. The brochure said it was healing, and she certainly needed some of that. When she described it to me, she said she was fully dressed and the provider never touched her. She could feel the energy from her hands moving throughout her body. She relaxed completely; amazed at what she was experiencing.

After the trip Dawn researched Reiki healing and found a class. She was amazed at what she felt and what others felt when working with her. Next she took a class reading Tarot cards, exploring the possibility that there is more to this life than we can see. Dawn was having a spiritual awakening just as I was. Could it be coincidental, that we were both individually experiencing an awakening at the same time?

We hadn't discussed any of this as it was happening. We were still learning about each other and building a relationship. Dawn came to stay at my house for the weekend to attend my granddaughter's christening. She met my mother, the rest of my family, and a few of my friends at the party. I imagine she must have felt a little uncomfortable during all of this, as I had when I'd gone to her mother's party. My cousins kept telling me how much we looked alike and that we had a lot of the same mannerisms. I invited the cousins back to my house afterwards and we had a good time. I also broached the subject of mediumship with Dawn. I asked her whether she believed that it was possible to communicate with those who had passed. She said she had never experienced it, but was open to the possibility. I told her that I had gone with Lauren and that I was amazed at the information the medium was able to provide. She told me about the Reiki and Tarot classes she had taken and said she felt there was definitely something to them; she was open to learning more.

I continued taking occasional classes at Montclair Metaphysical. I took a channeling class though I wasn't really sure what channeling was. It was interesting, and I easily entered a light trance state. The instructor explained our own personality is less present, and we allow spirit to come close to us and provide inspiration.

After that I took an Intuitive Tarot class. I had some previous experience with Tarot when I was younger but had never memorized the meaning of the cards. In this class the instructor suggested that we don't need to know the traditional meanings of the cards, but that we should react to the cards in an intuitive manner.

Finally, the school was offering Unfoldment into Mediumship in August of 2017. After my experiences in the psychic development class, I was ready to explore mediumship. It was a first level class for people who had never made contact with the spirit world before. It was a full weekend, so when I registered I also booked a room nearby. I was very excited for the class and could hardly wait for the day to arrive.

In one of the previous classes someone had mentioned a community in Lilydale, NY that was actually a town full of mediums. I was intrigued by the sound of it, and looked it up on the internet. I learned that it had originally been a spiritualist camp in the 1800s, and that many famous spiritualists had visited or spent time there. Today, many live there year round. To be listed as a certified medium in Lilydale there is a qualification process; each medium is tested prior to being listed as approved. I saw that there was a documentary on the town, and I found it and watched. I wanted to go there and hoped that Dawn would go with me. I called her to make the invitation.

Dawn was willing to go and I sent her a link to the documentary so she could watch. We wanted to go before the summer season ended with Labor Day weekend. We both went to the website and looked at the names of certified mediums as well as classes being offered. We settled on two workshops and chose two mediums and made the arrangements to spend Labor Day weekend in Lilydale. I didn't tell Dawn that I was signed up to take a mediumship class and I don't know why I didn't. While she had expressed an interest and was open to visiting a medium I wasn't sure how she would respond to my wanting to develop mediumship myself.

We were going to meet in the Catskills on Friday afternoon at Glenn's cabin, then drive together Saturday morning for the drive to Lilydale. The community is located in the western part of New York State, not very far from Buffalo. It would be close to an eight hour drive. We had a room booked in the Leolyn hotel since the guesthouses seemed to all be full already.

My Unfoldment class at Montclair Metaphysical was the week before my trip to Lilydale. My classmates and I were very excited when we arrived in the morning. Lee started out discussing the differences between mental mediumship and physical mediumship and explained this class was about mental mediumship. Lee talked about the objective to "serve the spirit world." She said the person there for the reading, the "sitter," was secondary. Our focus was on the spirit communicators so that we could become recommended by them. She told us that she had started her mediumship journey eleven years prior and that she was still learning and studying. She was in a mentorship with a famous British medium by the name of Mavis Pittilla, who I had never heard of before. In truth, I hadn't heard much about any famous mediums at that time, other than those on television. I had watched John Edwards a few times and the Long Island Medium Theresa Caputo, who was popular at the time. I read her book after my visit with Lauren to the medium who had unknowingly opened my desire to learn how to connect to spirit myself.

Lee talked about a book called *The Untethered Soul* by Michael Singer, which she had mentioned also in the Psychic development class. I had purchased and read it and was glad I had, as she mentioned it again. It was about how our ego can distort facts and control us and that we have a higher aspect within ourselves that we can reach, which Singer called the watcher, or observer. It wasn't such an easy read as the concepts were new to me, but I found it fascinating. Lee was using it to talk about the left brain, or ego mind, and the right brain where we use our imagination. She had named the voice of her ego mind "Frankie." She said that Frankie could torture her if she let it happen, and when she recognized that Frankie was talking she would switch to her imagination, or to the watcher who was detached from whatever the immediate situation was. We have to trust the process, she explained, and trust the spirit world. We would have good days and bad days on our mediumship journey.

We discussed identifying spirit in terms of evidence. Lee believed that we had to work with consistency and structure in the beginning until we'd gotten the hang of it. That meant asking to always receive specific evidence at the beginning of every reading, such as the gender of spirit while they were alive, and their relationship to the sitter. After that we might want to know the cause of passing, something of the spirit person's personality and maybe a shared memory, or proof of survival. Proof of survival is evidence the spirit is still around the sitter, and aware of what's currently happening in the sitter's life. She had an evidence chart on the wall with other types of evidence that we could choose to include in our structure.

We did a meditation where we pictured a column of white light coming down from the universe to surround us. We sat in the white light and allowed it to lift our vibrations and heal us. It was beautiful. Lee called this "sitting in the power" and told us we should be doing this at least twice a week on our own, for at least fifteen minutes each time. We could build the time we sat to half an hour as we continued. We could also do self-healing at other times, such as in the shower, where we could visualize the water as the healing light, which could be green. She also told us to journal and write our impressions and experiences with spirit every day. She explained that mediumship is active, and we must engage with spirit and to look for symbols in our work. We should build our own dictionary of symbols and what they mean to us. For example, mountains might mean challenges, or a sheep could symbolize someone is more of a follower, than a leader.

We started with photo readings, as we had been told to bring two photographs of someone in spirit world with us to the class. We swapped photos with a partner, then held each photo and wrote down our impressions from it, and then shared them. Surprisingly I got a few things correct in each round we did. Later we sat with partners and were supposed to connect to spirit for them. As I sat with my partner, I opened my mind to the spirit world and asked spirit to come to me.

I felt the presence of a young man with me, who was a relative. In my mind's eye I saw a boat in stormy seas and a sailor. I also felt a pressure in my chest. I shared these feelings with my partner. She said she had a cousin in the spirit world who had died of a heart related issue, and that he was a sailor in the navy. I was amazed at this, but instead of continuing I kind of froze up. I remember Lee walking around and telling us if we weren't receiving anything, to just make it up. She explained that spirit used our imagination to connect with us, and that just making it up was fine at this point. Through the rest of the class we continued this way, making it up if we didn't get clear impressions, and were pretty amazed at the number of things our partners could confirm as true. I was sad when the class was over, but also excited to continue. Lee gave us two certificates for her circle which met on Tuesday nights from 7:30 to 9:30 pm and told us that we could join in if we let her know when we wanted to come. I knew in my soul that I could do this.

FOURTEEN
LILYDALE

As I drove to the cabin to meet Dawn I thought about how my life had changed and continued changing. I was happier now that work was not as demanding as when I was doing arbitrations. I learned more about spirit and my psychic abilities and I was grateful and excited to get to Lilydale. We had booked a few workshops and two readings for each of us. One was to be evidential and the other was an aura reading with a drawing we could take with us.

We met at the cabin, which was really a small house near a ski resort in Ashland, NY. There isn't much to Ashland, except for its proximity to Wyndham, NY. Wyndham is a beautiful small town with a ski resort. The winter brought the skiers to the town and surrounding area. The town itself seemed quite busy, and we decided to go have dinner and then come back and relax. We were both eagerly anticipating getting to Lilydale. We left early the next morning in Dawn's car. She loved to drive and I was just as happy to let her.

The GPS on the car took us through the mountains and we saw some other beautiful small towns and some pretty poor and depressed ones. Some of the roads were a bit scary at times and I wondered if we should have ignored the GPS and headed for the NYS thruway before turning it on. It was a very long drive and we caught up on each other's lives as we went. We listened to the radio when we ran out of things to talk about, and complained about the other drivers on the road.

We arrived in Lilydale late in the afternoon. We paid for multi day passes for the weekend at the gate and the attendant pointed across the street to show us where our hotel, the Leolyn, was located. He then directed us to the Mayfair hotel, which is where we would check in. The town is small and full of interesting looking houses. Some looked like summer bungalows that had been refurbished for winter, and others were larger, old Victorian homes. All of them were on very small parcels of land. The houses are fairly close together, and the streets between them are narrow. It reminded me of where I grew up in Edgewater Park in the Bronx. Edgewater was a small private community located on Eastchester Bay. It had started as a summer camp, and the little cottages and bungalows had been winterized around the depression and people lived there full-time. I felt right at home in Lilydale, which was located on Lake Cassadaga.

The Mayfair Hotel was charming, though old, and looked to be in need of repair. There was some drama going on at the front with a guest who wasn't happy about something. We waited patiently to get our room key. The Leolyn was also charming and old when we entered. Our room however was threadbare and ancient. We had two beds, one full and one twin sized that were arranged in an odd way. We also had a private bathroom which was clean, but not very modern or inviting. We were there, and didn't want to start looking for somewhere else at that point so decided to make the best of it.

We had nothing planned for the evening but there was a program of events happening daily and we wanted to get to the stump where various mediums would be giving messages to the public. We walked across the street and back through the gate. We walked around with a map, looking at the different houses and shops as we passed them. The stump is set back from the road, in the Leolyn woods and is surrounded by very old and tall trees. There are rows of benches in front of the stump where people were already assembled and we sat towards the back. Neither of us got a message, but were impressed by the messages that some of the others received. We visited a couple of gift shops and spent what was left in the afternoon getting to know the town. We looked at the food establishments and chose a small outdoor place called Monica's. We ate and talked about our impressions.

There was a psychic development circle being held at 7pm and we decided to give it a try. We arrived and took seats in the hall but there was some commotion going on. As it turned out there was a film crew making a documentary. Lisa Ling was doing an episode of her series, *This is Life*, about Lilydale. The woman leading the circle announced this and told us we had to sign a waiver or permission slip to be there while they were filming. She said they would be as unobtrusive as possible and most people agreed and signed what was needed. It was an interesting way to start our weekend.

The next morning we had breakfast and talked about our upcoming readings. Dawn was hoping that her mom would come through, and I was hoping to hear from our father. We made our way to the house where we were to meet a medium named Patricia Bell. We rang the bell on the side door and after a moment or two she answered. She said that she would only read us one at a time, and the other one would wait outside in the small side yard. We told her we'd hoped to go in together, but she wouldn't budge. We decided to let Dawn go first, and I sat on a small bench outside. It was a beautiful day, and I decided to walk the tiny streets for a little while, rather than sitting there waiting. The time passed quickly and I made my way back to the house. As I was approaching the side yard, Dawn came out, rather quickly. She was in tears, and said "Go ahead, I told Dad to hang around, that you want to talk to him." I wanted to hear more, but went inside for my turn.

Bell talked to me for just a moment or two while I sat and got comfortable. She said that she had my father, and he was coming through with many regrets. She said he was raised in an unforgiving family who was strict in their ways, and he had also learned to live that way. She may have already known that Dawn and I were sisters; I wasn't sure what Dawn had already told her. She said I was born out of love, real love, but it was a whirlwind and that he had made his choices. He wanted me to know that he was glad I'd found Paul and Dawn.

Next, Bell had my grandmother. She said it was a woman who claimed me as a daughter. She described her as a very strong lady who had many hardships in life. The medium said she pushed her way through to tell me I never needed my father, and not knowing him had made no difference in my life. I chuckled, knowing that it was indeed Nana. She expressed her love for me and talked about my son, who had recently had a baby. She said that she was celebrating the baby with me. My father returned, and Bell said that he was around me quite often and was offering to help me from the spirit side. He wanted to support me since he hadn't when he was alive. She told me that she sensed that I was on a spiritual path, then asked if I was studying to be a medium. I acknowledged that I was just starting to do so. She said that my father would be available to me when I worked, and would help me if I let him.

Next, my brother Paul came through. The medium described him as my brother and that he was dancing around. He told her that Dawn and I were both too damn serious. He wanted us to have some fun. Bell said she felt that Dawn has been feeling like an orphan, and that we need to spend more time together. She also said we should travel overseas together. Ireland might be nice, she said, because we needed the whimsy. The time had flown by, and the reading was over.

I went out to meet Dawn and she asked me how it went. I gave her a summary of the reading. Dawn told me Bell had said that her father had been depressed at times. He kept himself from totally enjoying life and ignored his heart until it exploded. Dawn was stunned by the description. She told me that the lung cancer was killing our father, but that it was his heart that gave out. She'd been the one to find him, and it had indeed looked like his heart had exploded. She also said that our brother Paul was there, and told Dawn to stop blaming herself for his depression; there was nothing she could have done. Her mother had not come through the medium, but Dawn asked about her, and Bell said she was there with Dad and Paul. The readings had been very intense, and Dawn was quieter than usual. We decided to take some time alone and meet up in a little while.

We wanted to catch a healing service at the Healing Temple and messages were being offered that day at both the stump and the Forest Temple. We also had a couple of workshops and another reading, packing as much as we could into the short time there. The Healing Temple was calm and serene when we went in and took seats. The healers were all in the front sitting on chairs. As the service progressed, they stood behind them, and people in the pews could go up and take a seat in front of a healer. This was done in an orderly manner as the instructions given to all were clear. When it was our turn, Dawn and I went up and took seats. I was wondering how it would work, when the healer leaned down to ask in a whisper if he could touch my shoulders.

I agreed and then closed my eyes to relax. I found myself drifting into a slightly altered state of calm relaxation while the healer was working. His hands felt very warm on my shoulders and the warmth was spreading throughout my body. It seemed like I was there only a couple of minutes when the healer removed his hands and whispered a blessing, indicating that I should leave the chair so the next person could take it. I went back to my former seat and Dawn joined me a moment later. We sat a while longer, and then quietly made our way out.

We talked outside about our experience and Dawn's account was pretty similar to mine. We both felt pretty good. One of the main workshops we'd registered for had cancelled, so we had to go and try to arrange something else and ended up in a workshop on physical mediumship and trance. It was a fascinating lecture, slideshow and discussion by a Scottish medium.

In physical mediumship, the phenomena created by spirit can be seen and/or heard by anyone watching whereas in mental mediumship only the medium is aware of the communication. Physical mediumship is quite rare these days. We learned about apports and ectoplasm and saw old photos of mediums in various states of trance with ectoplasm shapes attached to them. Apports are physical objects which spirit has somehow made appear in the room through apportation. Spiritualists believe that spirit is able to dematerialize the item to be apported and is also able to rematerialize it in the room where it appears. Examples of objects which may be apported by spirit include crystals, stones, coins, feathers, and jewelry. Ectoplasm is a biological substance that exudes from the physical medium's body which spirit uses to create a likeness of the communicator during a seance. Ectoplasm is used by spirit for other purposes as well. In one slide during the presentation an apported crystal was squeezing out of the eye of a medium. I thought that was a bit too much and mentally noted to myself that I wanted nothing to do with physical mediumship.

When it was time for the aura readings, we went to the house of medium Sherry Lee Caulkins. She arrived home at the same time and invited us in. I was going first this time, and Dawn waited in a little seating area in the next room. Caulkins was a small, petite woman with long gray hair worn in a braid down her back. She told me that she would be drawing what spirit dictated to her and would talk to me as she went. She worked with colored pencils on a large 11" x 14" piece of paper and drew what looked like a large circle to start. She said that there were two angels in the room, the guardians of me and my father. She said that they were carrying someone out on a stretcher, and asked me if my father had been injured while he was in the service. I said I didn't know and she turned her head and spoke to spirit out loud, as though someone was right next to her giving her information. I found that odd and a little frightening. She said "Sometimes the angels have to save one life so that another soul can be born into the world." She indicated that this had been the case for me. She asked me if I had ever stopped breathing during a medical procedure or surgery. I said no, sure that I hadn't. She said I must have, because I have the Christ light around me.

"Sometimes they don't tell us what's happened while we're under anesthesia," she said.

She claimed that I had been saved a couple of times. She was drawing and shading her way around the circle she was drawing, talking about different periods in my life. When she was done, it looked like a coconut on the paper with various colors surrounding it. She then made her way around the drawing, explaining to me what the different sections signified. There were three indentations on the coconut. She told me that I had three children which was, of course, true. She talked about them for a moment saying that one of them was the source of more worry than the other two. She told me that he would have to find his own way, and that I couldn't control his path. She said that I had been born with the sac of amniotic fluid unbroken, so I was called a "caulbearer." I had a vague recollection of my mother telling me this once, that it was a dry birth and her water had never broken.

Caulkins talked about my intuition and said I would have success at whatever I want to do. She also said that I was ill as a child and that my recovery had been unexplained. This was also true. When I was two years old I'd woken one day screaming in pain. My mother said I had been walking quite well by then, but that day I couldn't stand or walk. She took me to the hospital and they kept me for weeks to figure out what was wrong with me. I was like a little parrot and would repeat whatever I heard from the adults around me. All the nurses loved me, and my mother talked about a doctor, Dr. Boris, who was elated when I finally said his name. Apparently he'd been trying to get me to say it for some time and when I finally did he'd gone out and boasted to all the nurses that I finally said it. My mother loved telling me that story whenever my medical history came up in conversation. They never confirmed exactly what had been wrong, but guessed it might be osteomyelitis, an infection in the bones. Just as suddenly as it came on, whatever it was disappeared and I was able to walk again. I told the medium about the mysterious illness and she nodded, knowingly.

Later Dawn told me about her reading and showed me her drawing. She said that there were several things Caulkins had said that were absolutely correct. We were both startled by the way she had spoken aloud to spirit. Dawn said she had thought the woman was nuts and we both laughed because I had the same thought. We talked about the weekend and I thanked her for coming with me. She said that she'd enjoyed it but if we came back we'd have to look for a nicer hotel outside of town.

We agreed there was definitely something to mediumship. We had both had several confirmations of the reality of the spirit world in our readings as well as watching the reactions of others in the services we'd attended. We talked for hours that night and got the giggles a few times. Sunday came so quickly we couldn't believe it. We drove back to the cabin and in the morning we had breakfast then said our goodbyes. We promised to keep in touch more often, as we always promised, and agreed to plan another trip soon. We had grown much closer that weekend, and would continue to do so.

FIFTEEN

CONFIRMATIONS

About five weeks after I took the *Unfoldment into Mediumship* class, Montclair was offering another class called *The Demonstrating Medium*. I had no idea what the class was about, but I figured it was mediumship, so I took it.

The first day I was a little nervous because I heard that some of the students had been going to her weekly circle for some time. She had us do readings with partners as well as individually in front of the class. I learned that when a medium did readings for a group of people it was called a *demonstration*, or a dem. She had us throw out a series of names and/or causes of passing in order to locate a sitter. We were to stand up and say, for example: I have a Mary, a James, someone who passed from a heart attack, and a Danny. If someone in the audience could take all of those names, and the cause of death then we should read for that person. It was actually fun once I'd relaxed with the group. We took turns doing this and it seemed to work all right. We didn't have to connect to anyone whose names we threw out, just work with the person who understood all of them.

Lee explained that spirit often comes in family groups and there is never just one spirit person present. Sometimes they come in other types of groups by occupation for example. She said that there could be a night where she got nothing but firemen or accountants. She told us it was good to try out different techniques that we could add to our repertoire as we continued to develop. On Sunday afternoon we were to individually demonstrate to a live audience of people that Lee had invited. We were all nervous about that. Sunday morning we practiced and Lee gave us feedback on the information we'd given and pointers on presentation. During lunch people went off in different directions to sit in the power before the dems. When the audience arrived we all sat in the front and Lee was the Master of Ceremonies. When I got up, I started just the way Lee had us do the prior day, by throwing out a series of names and causes of passing and asking who could take all of the information. Since only one person could take it all, I worked with her. As soon as I started, I felt a tingling all over my face, neck and shoulders.

"I have an older woman, here, who feels like your grandmother. I see her in her kitchen, which has older built-in white cabinets, and there is yellow paint on the walls." I asked if she understood that, and she said she did. I described her grandmother cooking in the kitchen, and then I saw a little girl with her long brown hair in two braids, sitting on a green carpet in the living room, in front of an old console television. She was playing jacks, trying to bounce the ball on the carpet and pick up the little silver jacks. I gave this information to the woman, telling her that I was seeing her through her grandmother's eyes, while I was standing in the kitchen. I told her how much love her grandmother had for her, and that I could feel it coming through me like a wave. I know I had some other evidence, but I don't remember it all as I am writing this. The woman accepted it all, and thanked me.

A man was there with me, and I felt the tingling again. I told the audience that I had a stocky gentleman with me, balding on the top of his head, who liked to sit outside his house in a lawn chair. He had a hearty laugh and a big heart and family was everything to him. I knew he was a father, and that he'd passed suddenly with a heart attack. A fellow student raised her hand. I worked with her for a few moments giving her additional details about her father some of which just dropped into my head and came out of my mouth. She said she understood all of it. It was really the easiest most natural thing in the world to stand there in front of those people like I did. I got tingles with every spirit person who came to me, and I trusted what they gave me.

My third contact was a woman, a mother who I described by her personality and appearance. One woman raised her hand for this one. I saw them walking in a park, and said that the daughter had fallen, and hurt her knee. She said that wasn't right; it was her mother who had fallen. I felt my knee hurting, and the back of my neck got numb and tingly at the same time. I said that when she fell, she'd also hurt her neck, and had some neurological problems as a result of that fall. The woman said that was correct. I don't remember what else I said, then my turn was over and I sat down. I couldn't believe how easy that had been. When the dem was over, the people in the audience were leaving and a few people told me that I had done really well. Lee gathered us together to give us feedback on the readings.

"Diane, you had balls to get up there and do the group readings. Congratulations for taking the chance." She said I did well and moved on to the next student. I was very happy and excited. Before we left I told Lee that I wanted to come to her circle. She told me it was full, but she could put me on a waiting list.

"I have two certificates for your circle," I said. She looked at me funny, and asked how long ago I'd earned them. "Maybe a month" I said, "six weeks tops."

"Are you shitting me? You were in the Unfoldment class at the end of August?" she asked.

I said "yes, that's right." She shook her head and said she thought I had been doing mediumship for a couple of years, at least.

"Ok, I'll put you down for the circle." I had been to the center a few times, but there had been other instructors I'd worked with. She remembered me, but didn't realize that I was brand new. I guess she sees a lot of students come and go. She was laughing and shaking her head.

I went to circle every week after that, although getting there from work was a bit stressful. There was tons of traffic going into New Jersey at 6 p.m. on weeknights. I kept a journal and would write what had happened each week when I got home. There were several professional mediums in the group so I was sometimes intimidated. I had good nights and not so good nights, which Lee said was normal. Occasionally I would have a really good reading. One I remember was for a woman who had been in the dem class with me, Lisa. I had her aunt who was showing me a white two story house. Inside, I described the living room and saw a spinning wheel. I gave her this information, doubting the entire time as I told her about the spinning wheel, thinking that it had to be my imagination. Lisa told me that it was her parent's house and they did have an antique spinning wheel in the living room. I couldn't believe it. I had stopped getting the tingles as I continued going to the circle; it happened only rarely after the dem class.

Lee had mentioned Mavis Pittilla a couple of times at the circle and I wanted to find out more about her. I went to her website and found that she would be starting an online mentorship program. I signed up for it right away. If Lee studied with Mavis, I wanted to study with her too. I saw there was to be a three day weekend workshop at a church in Pompton Lakes, New Jersey, in December. I had never been there, but had heard about it from the other mediums in the circle. I signed up for that class also. Before she would accept me into the mentorship program, Mavis wanted to meet with me on a Skype call. Her partner Jean made the arrangements and I was looking forward to the call. I was going to be in the office at the scheduled time so I brought my iPad to work and took lunch at that time.

Mavis and Jean came on together and Mavis asked me why I wanted to be a medium. I told her that I found it exciting and amazing; since finding mediumship I wanted to know more about the afterlife, and about God, and about everything. I said that it made me feel closer to God and that it made me feel good, knowing that there was life after death. I told her that I wanted to share that with others. She told me that I had beautiful colors in my aura, and that I had been a humanitarian all my life. She could see me defending people, she said, and then asked me what I do for a living. I told her that I defended teachers and other school personnel through the grievance process. Mavis asked me if I was a writer and I told her that I hadn't written for myself in a long time.

"You can do inspirational writing," she told me. She said that I could go far in mediumship and that I could be a public figure in this work. She said that I had been nudged towards this work for at least the past fourteen months. Mavis said she was pleased to have me join the mentorship program, and that Jean would fill me in on the practicalities. Jean told me that she had been an educator for most of her life, and that anyone who defended teachers was all right in her book. She went over the schedule and Facebook page information with me and welcomed me to the group. I told her that I'd signed up for the December workshop at the Journey Within. She was pleased and asked me to remind her I was in the online mentorship when we met in person. After the call I was very excited and eager to start working with Mavis.

The Journey Within is a Spiritualist Church run by Janet Nohavec, a well known medium in this country. She's a former Catholic nun and the author of two books; one about her life, and a mediumship guide book. She studied at the Arthur Findlay College in Stansted, England and is a tutor there as well. I read both of her books by the time I arrived at her church. The church itself is lovely, on a residential block in a building that formerly housed a Knights of Columbus Hall. When I entered the workshop, I signed in and went into the sanctuary where services are held. The high-backed chairs were covered in white slipcovers and set up in rows. I went to the second row and took a seat. Others were coming in and there was some excited chatter as we waited. I looked around at all of the beautiful artwork, much of which contained angels. I found it very peaceful sitting there.

Mavis and Jean entered the room and the workshop began. I love listening to Mavis's voice, it has a soft melodic quality to it. She talked about many of her opinions on the spirit world and mediumship as we began. Mavis believes that we are there to serve the spirit world rather than the sitter when we do mediumship. She wants us to learn to let spirit present the information that they want to, and do so freely. She does not believe that we should be making demands on the spirit world and expect to receive specific information per our requirements. I was thinking about how I was told to work with a consistent structure, and to ask that I receive the relationship to the sitter, personality, cause of passing and either a shared memory or proof of survival. Mavis was directly contradicting this approach and saying that we should not do that. We have to learn to trust the spirit world, and to talk to them. She said we should not rely on the sitter to validate the information but rely on the spirit communicator as we blend with them. She presented many opinions that expanded upon what I'd already learned. We then moved into practice sessions working with partners and small groups.

The following day's session was about myths and misconceptions and the difference between ghosts and spirits. It was fascinating. Later we talked about what she called *Worlds Within Worlds* which described the seven levels or worlds of Spirit. After that we did demonstrations and I saw that Mavis could link in with the same spirit that a medium was working with. As someone demonstrated, she would know what they were seeing or feeling, and also know what was missed. She gave feedback to each person and what she understood from spirit. I learned so much just from watching her work with my classmates.

When I got up to demonstrate, I communicated with a mother in the spirit realm, and I knew she had three children. She had passed from an illness and I felt a pulling sensation in my breast. I presented this information and saw two students raise their hands. I described the mom in front of her home and described a specific type of flower. Then I was left with only one sitter.

The spirit brought my attention to the month of June for her birthday, and that the sitter had done something to celebrate her mother's birthday. She said that she had. I saw the sitter in front of her mother's headstone, planting her mother's favorite flowers, the kind I had earlier described. For some reason, doubt then crept into my awareness. How did I know her mother was buried? She could have been cremated, or placed in a mausoleum. I did not want to say the word grave and instead said something like you went to the place where your mother is and planted those flowers for her. The sitter looked confused, but said she had planted flowers for her mother. Mavis stopped me and told me that I was judging too much of the information instead of just presenting it. She said "You saw her at the grave, but then you judged it, and got into your head." It was true, that was exactly what had actually happened. The sitter confirmed that she had planted those flowers at the grave for her mother's birthday. Mavis said that I had also missed the fact that the woman wanted to take me into her house, and show me around. She said I was not blending closely enough with the spirit, because I had missed that information. However, she was very pleased with what I did.

"You have to do this, and you know it," she said. "I would like to see you sitting for exams through the Morris Pratt Institute." I had no idea what that was and asked later. Jean mentioned that it was a correspondence course, so it differed from the way it was done in England, but that I could certify as a Spiritualist medium through them.

Afterwards, Mavis talked about how we are natural mediums when we start out, but when we start to attend development circles and workshops, sometimes we question ourselves. She said our mediumship would go through ups and downs as part of the experience. Eventually, the things we were learning would become natural to us, but we would struggle in the meantime.

I was in the online mentoring program and going to circles at Montclair, and reading everything I could on mediumship and spiritualism. I found the website for the Morris Pratt Institute (MPI), and read all of the information on how their program worked. I didn't know much about spiritualism, but I was ready to learn. If Mavis Pittilla wanted me to certify as a spiritual medium, then that is what I was going to do. Mavis had said that our words were very powerful, and I have often wondered if she knew just how powerful her words were in shaping what I would be doing in the few years that have followed. I signed up for the correspondence course with Morris Pratt and began learning. I was not a member of a spiritualist church at the time, and I discovered that I would need to join one and be a member for at least two years before I would qualify for any exams.

I started looking for churches in the National Spiritual Association of Churches (NSAC). I thought about the

Journey Within, which was a Spiritualist National Union (SNU) church. I liked the church but it took me at least an hour to get there from where I lived in the Bronx. I didn't think I would want to commit to attending regularly if I had to drive so long to get there and then again to get back. I started working on the Morris Pratt lessons. The first was about the advent of Modern Spiritualism and the Fox Sisters. Mavis had said that we had to learn about the "pioneers" of spiritualism, and Lee had asked people to research pioneers and present to the group what we had learned. I listened to a presentation on the Fox sisters before I started the MPI program, so I had a little familiarity with their story from that presentation.

As I progressed through the first few lessons, I realized that there was a structure to most of them; they started with the historical, moved into the present and looked at implications for the future. There are 30 lessons in total for the full course, which aren't all needed to certify for NSAC Medium. Some pertain to healing and the others to the ministry. The paperwork said I would have five years to complete the course. That sounds like a long time, but the lessons have sometimes 30 or more questions and then you have to write an essay to summarize each lesson. It is slow going and I have been taking the course for three years. I opted to take the full course, and I am currently at lesson 25 I think. I am almost at the end..but not quite.

There was a spiritualist church in Manhattan that I read about online. I also saw on the NSAC website that there is a church in Old Greenwich, Connecticut. In June of 2018, I visited Albertson Memorial Church of Spiritualism for the first time. It was about 30 minutes to the church by car, which was doable. I attended a service, which I enjoyed.

Prior to the healing, they led those in attendance through a guided meditation. I loved this part. There was what they called "fellowship" downstairs after the service. Everyone was welcoming and one woman actually hugged me. I stayed for the coffee and fellowship and spoke to a few people. That day there was a special workshop after the fellowship on Metaphysics and Spiritual Development. The session gave an overview of a course on "Jacob's Ladder" which was very interesting. We sat in a circle after the lecture and a gentleman led a meditation. It was awesome. The energy in the room was palpable; I could feel it rolling over me in waves, and across the upturned palms of my hands. The class was going to start in the fall, and I knew that I would want to participate. After that, I attended regularly.

SIXTEEN
ARTHUR FINDLAY COLLEGE

At the end of July I flew to England to spend a week at the famed Arthur Findlay College. I'd heard Mavis speak about it many times, and one of the mediums from the circle at Montclair had a fantastic experience there. I went to the website and saw a course on Spiritual Development and Mediumship with Colin Bates as the lead tutor. I signed up and booked my airfare. It was the first time I had traveled to Europe on my own. I had been to England once before, with a group of people from work and my friend Samantha. We'd spent a few nights in London before getting on a cruise ship at Southampton for a British Isles Tour. It had been one of the best trips I'd ever taken.

This time, though, I would not be touring. I was landing on Saturday morning at 9:30 a.m. and had to make my way to Stansted, a good hour by car from London. The course started on Saturday, and ended the following Saturday. I had a return flight booked for Saturday evening. I heard that I could take a train from Heathrow to Stansted, but I was nervous about getting lost and traveling with luggage on my own. I booked a car service instead, which was a bit expensive but worth it in my opinion. The driver picked me up at the airport and drove me right to the door of Stansted Hall. I entered the small reception area and saw suitcases all over the room. The receptionist checked me in and told me I could leave my luggage along with the rest until the rooms were ready. She said to come back in the afternoon at about 3 p.m. for my room assignment. I walked around the building which was spectacular. It was old, and some of the furniture was in need of repair, but the atmosphere was incredible. I was so excited and happy to be there.

I walked through the main hall and then through a little corridor that had photos of all of the tutors on one wall. It led past the dining room and continued into the lounge and bar area. There were people sleeping in the lounge, on the sofas and on the chairs. I went outside and sat on the large lawn, noticing how beautiful the manicured grounds were. There were horses that approached the wall that separated the main garden from the neighboring property. The horses were coming up to the students at the wall, who were offering apples or carrots to them. Watching this scene made me very happy.

At 3:00 I went back and stood in line (or queue as they referred to it) waiting for my room. I was in a single room in an annex they called the cottage, down a path beyond the great lawn. I found my way there and got settled into the room. I had a small sink, but no toilet or shower. I would have to use the common bathrooms outside in the hall, and that was fine. There was a welcome session at 5 p.m., then dinner. We were warned that we had to keep our seat in the dining room once we chose one. Meals were served buffet style and people lined up outside, then took a tray for food once in the dining room. I was walking and looking around, not knowing where to sit. A table with a group of ladies my age waved me over. I joined them and we all introduced ourselves. They were all English, except for one woman who was from Wales. They were funny and friendly and I was feeling comfortable with them. The other students were from all around the world; Spain, Germany, Italy, Sweden, China, Japan and Australia. After dinner there was a meditation session with Bill Thompson and I fell asleep in the middle of it. It was dark when I made my way back to my cottage. The walk was a bit scary to me, through the trees on a little path. There were light posts, but as a New Yorker I wasn't feeling very safe. I was fine once I got to my room and I slept like a rock.

Our groups were posted in the little corridor opposite the photographs in the morning. Everyone was checking the wall to see where they had been placed. We were assigned to one tutor for our groups, but would have sessions with the others as well. I was assigned to Colin's group. I couldn't believe it. He was the course organizer and apparently everyone wanted to be in his group. The other tutors were all well known mediums: Sandie Baker, Simone Key, Bill Thompson, John Johnsom, Mia Ottosen and Lynn Probert. My understanding was that you couldn't really go wrong no matter which group you were put in. The experience brought to mind the "sorting hat" in the Harry Potter novels. I had read them all, devoured them as they came out. I realized that this was the real life Hogwarts. J.K. Rowling must have been a student at the college, I guessed.

Each day we worked in our groups for two sessions, and then the other sessions were with other tutors. Colin's group met in the sanctuary. We did lots of exercises and experimented with different techniques. The energy in the sanctuary and throughout the college is phenomenal. I believe that there is such a concentration of spirit in Stansted Hall, that as mediums we can reach new heights while studying there. Spirit seems to want to show us what we are capable of in this magical place. I did well in almost all of my readings, and I had a few really incredible experiences. Each night after dinner there was something in the sanctuary that we all attended. One night there was a service, and demonstrations on other nights. Afterwards, people would meet in the bar and lounge area. It was a younger crowd, but there were plenty of people my age, and older as well. I went each evening and enjoyed the music, and the laughter. We were busy night and day and I loved it all. We were able to sign up for readings or spiritual assessments if we wanted them. I wanted an assessment from Colin, but his line was full and he was booked up. I signed up for one with Sandie Baker, and for an auragraph with Mia Ottosen.

In the group work Colin pushed me to blend more with the spirits I was working with. On Monday, I met with Sandie for my assessment. She said that she was a "tell it like it is" person, and that she would be very honest with me. I was good with that, and she began. She said that I was a healer, and that if I wanted to develop it, mediumship was certainly possible for me. She said I had a calming, healing energy, and that people would love to come to me for private sittings. She also said that I was alone in my mediumship and very determined. I agreed that she was right on that. I recorded the session and listened to it several times over. My energy was very passive, she said, which was great for healing but not so great for mediumship. I would have to be more active and work at lifting my energy. She also suggested that when I came back to the college I should stay a few weeks in order to get more instruction. I liked that idea. She wasn't the only person to tell me I was a healer that week. I had taken Reiki levels one and two by then at Montclair. I liked the class, and knew that there was a power working with me when I did it. However, healing wasn't what I wanted to focus on. I really wanted to focus on mediumship.

Colin had us do demonstrations in our groups. As each person got up, I marveled at how good they were. What had made me think that I was ready to be here? When my turn came, I decided to relax and allow myself to let go. As I turned my mind to spirit, I knew I had a mother with me. I saw her outside, hanging clothes on a clothesline. I knew she worked hard for her family, and felt that she had sons. I also felt that the home was out in the countryside. I knew that this mother was very sad. There were dogs at her feet, two of them that I could see. As I gave this information, none of the students could identify the woman, but Colin said that he could. He told me to go on. I knew that this mother was sad, and was going through bouts of depression. I knew that she was left alone with the children. I said I was trying to see how many children she had, and Colin stopped me.

"Don't go looking for anything... just let her give you what she wants."

I said that her husband had left her, and that she was struggling to deal with it. I said she could be cross at times because of this. Colin said that wasn't right, and I needed to stay there. Instead, I responded that sadness could come out as anger, and that this woman had indeed been going through all of these emotions. Colin told me to move on from that. I said that she had been a joyful and kind woman and that she loved music. The information was just coming to me at that point, and I know I used clairvoyance, as well as clairsentience and claircognizance. Colin challenged me to go deeper with the music.

"What kind of music did she like?" he asked.

I stopped and closed my eyes for a moment and I heard a song in my head. It was from Disney's Little Mermaid. It had no words and was just a series of notes with a woman's voice singing, "Ah, a, ah, Ahh, a, ah."

"I hear it. It's a Disney song, from the Little Mermaid," I said, and sort of sang the notes.

As I was about to continue, Colin interrupted me, "That's right!" he exclaimed. "She loved Disney. Is there anything else?" he asked.

I had been stopped by the excitement in his voice and was suddenly self-conscious. As I was about to answer, I heard another song. This time it was "Be our Guest" from Beauty and the Beast, the song where the little candlestick and the teacups are all singing. Instead of giving this information, I said "No, that's all" and sat down.

"My mother loved Disney, but she never got to go to Disney World. I am going for the first time later this year." As he said that, I realized what she had been trying to tell me, with the second song. I didn't say anything, however. I was glad that I wasn't still standing and looking at the group. Colin said "well done" and then the next person got up.

I sat there asking myself why I hadn't given the second song. I knew if I had, I would have said that someone was going to Disney World soon. I hadn't been studying long, but knew at that point that if I withheld information, I would screw up the contact. Yet, I still did it. I recalled Mavis telling me to stop judging the information and just give it. This was an ongoing challenge for me but I was pleased at the fact that I'd gotten claraudience for the first time. I wanted more of that faculty.

Colin told us that he had paired each of us up with another student in the class, but that he would not be telling us who. For homework, we were to think about that person while in the power, and write about their journey. Then, we would share if we felt that we knew who it was. This was a two day assignment, and I toyed with it in my head throughout the next day. I decided that I was paired with Sanya, a lovely young woman who I believe was from Spain. I thought about her, and wrote what I felt as I did. When it was time to share, Colin asked first if anyone thought they knew who they were paired with. I didn't say anything. I was still self-conscious and nervous and I kept the information to myself. A few people volunteered, some were correct, and some were not. Colin did not look at me, but said again "Anybody else?"

I felt like he was waiting for me to speak up, but again I didn't. When he told us who we were paired with, I found out that I had been correct; it was Sanya. I regretted not speaking up, but congratulated myself at the same time. I didn't say anything at that point because it was too late. I shared what I had written with Sanya, and she said it was pretty accurate. What she had written about me was also.

I was in a workshop later that day when a student got up and said they had to leave because they had a reading scheduled. It dawned on me that I did also, and was already late for my auragraph reading with Mia Ottosen. I had completely forgotten about it. I got up and hurried towards the room where I was to meet her, and knocked on the door. She told me to come in. I apologized for being late, and she said not to worry about it. She had started on my little picture already. She told me that she starts with two main colors. Green and turquoise were the two colors she chose for me and she told me that they were in my aura. She said that I had healing abilities and was used to letting other people's needs take priority over my own.

"Be a little more selfish and a little more egotistical," she said. These qualities were not evident in my aura, she explained, and said that I needed to cultivate them. She talked some more about my healing energy and said that healing will come through everything that I do.

"You are stubborn and don't give up easily. You are also independent, sometimes too much so. You don't like to ask for help. I can see that you know who you are, and have done some spiritual development. However, you tend to be too critical of yourself, and don't always see the good things about yourself or the things you have done. Be more positive and celebrate what you do get in your mediumship instead of always looking at what you missed."

As she spoke to me, she continued working on the little auragraph. She used an iron to melt some material, like a wax and pressed it to the paper that she held. What she was saying rang true for me. She said I need to brainwash myself into being positive and that I can be too ethical at times. If I think I might be making it up, I don't share what I think, but I need to trust the intelligence of the spirit world. She talked about pink and gold and orange in my colors, and said that my mind interferes in my mediumship. She said that I should trust, and when the information slows down, to start a new sentence like "I also know that..." and that something else will come. I should just keep talking and trust what comes. I will build my confidence as I go, she said. She produced a beautiful auragraph with lots of green for healing and I was thrilled with it. It was beautiful and I was glad I went. As I was leaving, she said that I was versatile and wouldn't be satisfied with just focusing on mediumship.

Lynn Probert did a workshop about the power of our words. She said that the words we use can empower our mediumship or disable it. Spirit comes with a purpose and our words can stimulate the information. She encouraged us to experiment with the words and phrases we are using in our mediumship. If we see a pile of notes, for instance, and we've given that information, we can stimulate more by saying "As I look at this pile of notes..." and something will come to us. I thought how scary that sounded. To just start to talk and hope the rest of the sentence got filled in by spirit. That really does require trust. Mia has said something similar in my reading with her. I enjoyed the session and Lynn's teaching style and energy. She also did a session on nurturing the medium, which was all about understanding ourselves and being kind rather than critical. She is down to earth and responsive to the questions of her students. I decided after her sessions that I would like to study with her some more, and thought that I would look for her courses when I came back again.

I learned so many things while I was at the college. Colin believed that we should not go looking for information in a contact, but that we should allow the spirit to communicate as they liked. We should take what comes to us, what *they* want to show us, and then go deeper into that information, rather than *trying* to get something or other. I can still remember some of the contacts I had with the spirit world while I was there; it was so easy for me to connect with them. I remember working with a man named David, who looked so much like a boy I had grown up with. I got his grandmother and I saw her out in a garden, virtually surrounded by plants. I knew that she was a wise woman and understood how each of the plants and herbs could be used as remedies for healing.

I also saw a family tree, and knew that she was the family historian and had been proud of the family history. I sensed that David was also interested in ancestry and that he had spent some time researching the family history. He affirmed all of the information that I had given him. It was an absolutely wonderful week and I didn't want to leave. The ladies I sat with in the dining room had become friends during the course of the week and I was sad to leave them also. We vowed to keep in touch and to plan on coming back at the same time in the future.

SEVENTEEN
HEALING

After I joined Albertson Church I felt like I had found a community of people who understood me. I enjoyed the services and chatting with people during fellowship afterwards. The metaphysics and spiritual development class started in the Fall of 2018 and I attended on Tuesday nights. We were supposed to spend time meditating each morning on a specific phrase that was related to a lesson we'd been given. One week we would discuss and explore the lesson, and the following week we sat in a circle and asked spirit to join us.

I had many great experiences in those sittings and found myself getting deeper and deeper into a trance like state during them. However, I was almost always pulled back by something or someone saying my name in the circle.

I became more interested in healing at this time. At Albertson all services started with hands-on healing. I wondered how I could participate in that, and asked someone after service. I found out that to be a designated healer I would have to take a two session class from

Reverend Jackie Randall. One of the ladies who was in the Tuesday night classes told me that she had taken the first part, but missed the second and they were inquiring about whether she would come back and do it again. They wanted her to do both sessions in a single day to get more people qualified to do healing in the church. She agreed and I attended the class.

We were a pretty small group of five women. Reverend Randall went over decorum and ethics, reminding us never to put our hands near any sensitive areas or body parts, and telling us that sticking to the shoulders was best. We should be dressed appropriately for church service and shouldn't wear perfumes that might irritate or cause a reaction in some people who sat for healing. We were told not to give messages during healing and not to diagnose anyone. She had us practice scanning the body to try to sense what might be bothering a person. We then had to scan her, and tell her what areas we felt were an issue. I focused on her head and worked my way down to her toes. I sensed that she had headaches, shoulder pain and trouble with her right leg and foot. I also felt something in the area of her pancreas. We each had to tell her what we'd felt. She confirmed some things and told us where we were totally off, but did not give feedback on everything. She told me that I was doing pretty well. At the end of the class she gave us certificates and we were now allowed to do healing at services.

I enjoyed doing healing. I would connect with whoever was sitting in the chair and just ask spirit to work with me to send healing to the person. Sometimes I would imagine the energy entering my crown and moving down through me into my arms and my hands. It was pleasant for me and the sitters seemed to get something from it. There were usually more healers available than chairs for healing, and the way it worked was whoever got to a chair first was able to do the healing. There were many times that I would head for a chair only to have another healer arrive there before me or at the same time. I would always move away and let the other have the spot. Some of the other new healers and I started strategically planning our seats for service so as to be close to a healing chair.

In April of 2019 I returned to Arthur Findlay College during the Spring Break. I was itching to get back there for the week of Trance Healing with Matthew Smith as the course organizer. I wasn't familiar with Matthew, but Colin Bates and Sandie Baker were also teaching that week and I decided to go. I had no real experience with trance but wanted to learn more about it, and I was definitely interested in learning more about healing. This time, I booked my flight to leave on Thursday night and arrive Friday morning, a full day before the course was to start. I wanted to be well rested by Saturday when we started.

I booked a small bed and breakfast in the town of Stansted and knew that I could walk front there to the school on Saturday. There is an airport in Stansted, but I couldn't seem to find any flights from New York that went there. On my previous trip I had walked into town with some of the ladies and they had shown me where the train station was. They said it would be easy to take the train from Heathrow, and I toyed with the idea a bit, but booked the car service again in the end. I was still nervous about taking the trains with my luggage and not being sure of exactly what trains I needed. The car took me directly to the bed and breakfast, and I checked into a lovely room with a private bath. I was happy with my choice and decided to go out and walk around the town for a while to be sure I could find my way to the location of the road that led to the college. It wasn't really a road, it was more like a driveway that led from the school's reception area past some fields and then between two houses before intersecting with the town road.

I wandered around for some time, trying to get my bearings when I saw the train station. I made my way from there and found the entry. I walked up the hill to the school to be sure it was the right place. It was, and I looked at the school for a moment, before turning back into town. There is a castle in the middle of the town that is open to the public. I headed towards it, thinking maybe I would pay a visit since I hadn't when I was last here. It was open, but I decided that I was hungry and needed to eat. I walked back to the bed and breakfast, which had a pub two or three doors down that was recommended for a quick bite when I'd checked in.

There were some people sitting on a patio outside enjoying the sun and a pint. Inside it was pretty quiet. I saw a table in the corner and claimed it then walked up to the bar and got a beer. I told the gentleman there that I'd like to order some food, and he gave me a menu and said he'd send the waitress over. I wanted something traditionally English, to celebrate my return to that country. I ordered a beef pie that looked interesting and came with some salad. It was quite a large meal and I dug in. It must have started raining, because a bunch of people came in and took seats at the surrounding tables.

Two older gentlemen saw me sitting alone, and asked if they might join me. I welcomed them and they sat and introduced themselves. I can't remember their names, but they were brothers. One lived next door to the pub and the other was from a neighboring town. They told me that they liked to get together fairly often, and this was where they usually met and spent a few hours. The gentleman who was not from the town said that he'd been dropped off and would be picked up by his daughter since he certainly wouldn't be driving after being in the pub all day. They were very pleasant and I stayed much longer than I would have if I was on my own. One of them laughingly commented on my meal "you don't worry about your figure, I see."

I laughed and said I was hungry and celebrating my arrival. They asked why I was in town, and I told them that I was attending the college. They exchanged glances, and asked me to tell them what I would be studying for the week. I told them about the course and that I was a medium and had been here the previous year. I think one of them thought I was crazy, but the other seemed more open and interested in life after death and mediumship.

Eventually, two young ladies entered the room and came over to join us. It was the daughter and a friend who came to pick up her dad. Her father introduced us and filled them in on the conversation. He got them each a drink and got one for me as well. They were interested in hearing about the school and both seemed open to discussing the spirit world. They had only one drink and said that they had to go. We all parted company and I went back to my room. It had been a nice couple of hours and I was a bit tipsy and ready for bed. In the morning, I had breakfast alone in the little dining room, then went back to my room to shower and make my way to Stansted Hall. I had no trouble finding the road again, and arrived a few minutes later, which was still too early for room assignments. I went to the desk and asked if I could upgrade to a private room, if one was available. I wanted to be in the main building this time, and had booked a shared room.

The woman said that I was in luck; they were under-booked for the week since another course had canceled. She could give me a room to myself, that had a private bath. It was meant for three people, but she wouldn't have any problem not filling it up. I was happy and said that it would be wonderful. I left my luggage and walked through the building and out the other side to the great lawn. It was a beautiful day, and this time I'd packed a small airplane blanket in my pocketbook. I went to the middle of the lawn and spread it out, so I could sit on it and enjoy the sun and the day. I lay there for a while, thinking about how happy I was to be here, and how grateful I was that I could afford to make this trip again. I allowed the energy of the place to sink into my very being and relaxed.

The course organizer, Matthew, is a very funny character. When the full group met for the first time in the Sanctuary, he had most of us laughing and giggling. The course was organized in a similar way to the last course I had been on. We would work in groups primarily, but then meet with the other tutors at various times during the upcoming week. We would be able to book healings with a few of the tutors, as well as get evidential readings or spiritual assessments. Our group assignments were posted in the hallway the next morning, and I would be working with Sandie Baker. I was happy with that, since I was acquainted with her from my last trip. The week was very interesting and very different from the mediumship week. Sandie started us out by having us sit and try to attain a trance like state. Afterwards, she asked each of us to describe our experiences. Everyone said something different: they had seen colors, or eyes, or people, or had traveled to different places. When we were all done, Sandie told us that while we'd each had a nice experience, none of us had been in trance. She explained that all of the things we saw were evidence of an overactive mind. We would need to learn how to quiet our minds if we wanted to do trance healing. The group was quieter after that.

Sandie instructed us on how to begin and it was certainly a struggle for me. Almost every class began with us sitting in the silence, attuning to the spirit world. We did this by clearing our minds, as best we could and then asking our healing guides to join us. This was quickly becoming a totally different experience from the mediumship week. We spent the largest proportion of our time in a passive state, sitting with spirit. While people did go to the bar at night, it was a quieter crowd and everyone left earlier. We learned about Mesmeric passes to assist others with attaining the trance state, and in a session with Andrej Djordivitch, we learned that we could purposefully take ourselves out of our minds by occupying them. The concept is harder to explain, but if we give the mind something to do or focus on, we can free up space for spirit to work through us. He led us through this in a guided meditation that was similar to some of the guided meditations I had already been doing.

I found this technique to be easier than trying to clear my mind and I adopted it immediately. In one session with a different tutor we sat in silence again. However, when I came out of it, I felt someone standing behind me. I knew it was spirit, and I knew it was a woman. As I realized this, I also realized that the class had moved on. They were talking about a child that had come through and discussing things that I had taken no part in. The session was nearly over and

I had completely missed it. I was a bit confused and dazed, but realized that I had not been present in the room. I should have gone to the instructor and explained what had happened to me, but I didn't. I was very tired and didn't have the energy to do anything. It was dinner time, so I made my way to the dining room. My table mates for this class were all nice people, and I felt better after eating and chatting with them. I still wonder where I went during that class, but I have no memory of it.

We did partner work throughout the week and I felt the healing I received each day through our exercises. I was getting deeper into the trance state and others told me that they could feel the healing energy from me pretty strongly. I booked a healing session with Andrej. I had to bring a partner with me so I asked Annette, a woman in my group to join me. She sat as an observer, something we were told we always needed when doing trance healing.

I could feel myself going into an altered state as I received healing from Andrej's healing guide. I was relaxed and open. The healer spoke to me through Andrej; he said that he was sending energy and prayer that I would have the strength to make the decisions I had to make. Then the session was over, and I felt pretty good. I spent some time wondering what decisions I had to make, but wasn't sure what he had meant. Annette said she felt like she was going into an altered state also, just watching the session. Sandie had mentioned in our group that Matthew's healing was really pretty special so when Matthew announced at dinner that night that he still had one or two spots left if anyone else wanted to book a session with him, I took one.

This time I asked another classmate Linda to attend with me. Matthew took some time to get into the trance state, then got up and stood behind me. The energy was flowing through me, and I went into a sort of trance as well. He continued moving around me as I sat there, tears streaming down my face for some reason. He started speaking, and I could hear him, but I didn't understand what he was saying.

He said my name, and asked me to come back. When I opened my eyes, he spoke again. He said that spirit connected with me easily, since I had led a prayerful life. He told me that the healing would take place over several days, and to be kind to myself. I might be more emotional than usual, he said, and to expect that. I looked over at Linda, and realized that she had tears in her eyes as well. When we left she said she was very moved by the session, and that she could feel the energy where she was sitting. It was very special.

By the end of the week, I was feeling comfortable with Trance Healing. I was blending with spirit very easily having done it many times each day that week, and I was very happy I had come. As a group we had watched demonstrations of trance and inspired speaking and were encouraged to return in October for a trance healing part two. Many of my classmates said that they would be returning, but I knew I wouldn't be able to with my work schedule. The week was over too quickly and I was home. I found that I was calmer and had a bit more confidence in myself than I had before that week of healing. I would feel myself blending with spirit without even trying, which was nice, until it happened while I was driving my car one day. I felt the rush of spirit surrounding me and the blending begin, and I got nervous being that I was behind the wheel. I thought "No" emphatically, and communicated that it was not the right time. After that, the spontaneous blending stopped. I often wonder if it was a mistake to have stopped it.

I incorporated what I'd learned into my hands on healing in the church and found it worked very well. A light altered state is sufficient for spiritual healing which, I learned, is what trance healing is. I was focusing more on my healing at the time than on evidential mediumship. I was thinking that I could just work with healing and make that my total focus as I was driving to work one morning. As I did, a car with a vanity license plate indicating the driver was a golfer passed me. I thought I could even get license plates with HEALER on them. A second after I had that thought, I saw a car go by with "EGO 2468" on the plate. I laughed out loud, and took that as a sign that I was getting carried away with myself. Spirit works in mysterious ways, which leads me into the next chapter.

EIGHTEEN
THE BIG PICTURE

Part of me always knew, deep inside, that I would do this work. Mavis said I was nudged towards mediumship. I believe it was my own soul that nudged me towards this path. I ignored it and dismissed it through most of my adult life. My higher self, my soul, has been trying to get my attention since I was a child. It is difficult to be a medium without trying to understand the spiritual world and the bigger picture. Why are we here? Is there a God?

Mediumship is the gateway to the spiritual path. Of course, that doesn't mean that you have to become a medium to be on the path, but a reading from a good medium can start you on it. Skeptics who don't believe in life after death, may have to reconsider if one of their own loved ones speaks to them through a medium. That is the purpose of evidential mediumship; the sitter should know that their loved one is indeed communicating because the medium couldn't possibly have known the information any other way.

The internet and Facebook have caused problems in mediumship. There is a great deal of information available online about people these days. Skeptics will point to this in an attempt to discredit mediumship in general. There are unscrupulous people who bill themselves as mediums who will use social media to get information about potential sitters. That is why the evidence is critical. Physical descriptions and general information do not suffice. Mediums need to bring the personality of the spirit person, and shared memories that can't be found on the internet.

As human beings, we want to know who we are in the world, and where we are going. Our identities are very important to us. We are the children of our parents, and they shape the identity we adopt as we grow. We are socialized to believe certain things about ourselves.

We believe we are good at math, or that we are hopelessly uncoordinated and not athletic through the experiences we have and how they are reflected back to us by our parents. Not all of us grow up secure in our identities, knowing who we are or what we want to do in the future. Some people undergo years of therapy before they feel that they know and understand themselves, and others never get to that level of understanding.

As a medium, I have been told over and over again by my teachers that I need to understand myself, deal with my own demons and see myself objectively in order to be a clear channel for spirit. While I am actively engaging in the work, I also need to understand my own soul. While we are here in this physical life, we forget who we are on a soul level. We believe what we've been taught and accept the world's view of who we are. In order to know who we really are, we have to unlearn what we've been taught about ourselves. Only then can we discover why we are here; our soul's purpose.

I believe that there is a universal energy that is divine; we are all expressions of that energy and we carry it inside of us. This is what we call God. I am a soul living in a physical body at this moment in time, but I will leave it when this life is done. My soul will not cease to exist when my body is gone. I will still exist. I will be me, with my own memories and personality when I transition to the spirit world.

I believe that my soul will keep evolving and learning and may return to the physical world again if there are more lessons to be learned. That's why we come into this world; to learn something. We choose our parents and our birth circumstances and put ourselves into situations designed to teach us some specific lesson.

Unfortunately, once here we forget what that lesson is. We see this life from birth to death as all there is to reality. Reality is so much more than this life. Our souls know reality. I have to understand my soul to understand my purpose.

Synchronicities are significant and meaningful signs from the universe, spirit world, or God. I have found many synchronicities on my spiritual path.

When I decided to look for my father and found my brother Paul on Facebook, I knew in my soul who he was just by looking at his photo. He read my first message and responded to me on my father's birthday. I don't think that was a coincidence; it was a sign. Dawn, Paul and I were all born under the astrological sign of Leo. All summer babies; coincidence? I'm not sure.

Then there's Dawn's best friend Lisa who was born on August 18. They are more like sisters than friends. My best friend Liz was also born on August 18, and we have always been more like sisters as well. I guess it could be another coincidence, but I don't think so.

My father wrote poems and short stories just as I used to do in my younger days. In almost every professional mediumship reading I've ever had, I was told by the medium or by spirit that I am supposed to write a book. Actually, I had an astrological chart done by one of my teachers when I was in 7th grade, and she said that I was supposed to write. I wrote short stories and essays all the time at that age. I'm finally writing again, as I believe I was always meant to do.

Sometimes spirit communicates through music. I have had songs give me information on several occasions, like when I had my tutor's mother in spirit and heard the Disney songs. Before I sold my house and heard the voice tell me " it's Marianna's house now," I kept hearing the old Ethel Merman song, *Everything's Coming Up Roses*. These are signs that I now pay attention to when they happen. As I wrote this book I had an old Bobby Goldsboro song stuck in my head. The song was *Honey,* and it was about a man who had lost his wife and was mourning her. I hadn't heard it recently, on the radio or in a television show, so there was no reason for it to be playing over and over in my head. As I was writing about Dawn showing me my father's stories, I remembered the book she had made for me, and I went and got it out. I sat and reread it and found the story that had made me feel like he was writing about me. The title of the story was "Honey." The song was a sign, meant to get me to reread the story.

NUDGED BY SPIRIT

Spirit influences us in subtle ways, and we usually don't even realize it. I have come to understand that I was influenced by spirit to seek my father. Moreover, I now understand that it was my father who influenced me to look in the first place. I believe that from the other side we know our life plan and how some events will unfold after we've gone.

My father wanted me to find Dawn. He knew that Paul would be joining him soon, and he knew that Carol wouldn't be far behind. He regretted not claiming me as his daughter, and he also didn't want Dawn to be left all alone. I know there's one other reason Dawn and I were meant to know each other. I don't know what that is yet, but it will unfold in time. For now, I am content to know her, love her, and call her my sister.

Before finding Paul and Dawn, I thought life was about making enough money to live comfortably, taking care of my children and taking a vacation every year. I had no great passions. Finding my siblings led to finding mediumship and finding my own soul.

My life has changed in many ways over the years. I went from living with my mother to getting married, having kids, then getting divorced. I was in a long term relationship for twenty years after my marriage so I was never really on my own. I am not afraid to be alone anymore. I am now, and actually prefer it. Two years ago I ended my relationship with Glenn because I knew I had to be alone in order to do what I needed to do. We had our ups and downs, but ending that relationship was hard.

I am hopeful for another partner in my life in the future, but for now I'm content with my connection to the spirit world, and serving them. I still work for the union, but will be retiring soon. Then I'll serve spirit full-time and continue my explorations on this spiritual path. That is where my passion lies. I am still unlearning and eliminating the limited beliefs I once held about who I am. I know that I can do anything I set my mind to, and you can too.

NINETEEN
FINDING YOUR OWN CONNECTIONS

Now that you've heard how I found my connection to spirit, you may be wondering how you can find your own. Many people feel the influence of spirit, although they don't recognize it as such. These are people who appear to be very gifted in their field of work; the musicians, painters, artists, authors, surgeons, physicians, teachers, counselors, carpenters, etc. They are intuitive and inspired and passionate about whatever they do. They get into a mental zone or flow when they work, and they follow the ideas that come to them.

I believe that these people are inspired by those in spirit who were experts in their chosen field while they lived. The more open they are to their own intuition and soul, the easier it is for spirit to influence them, in my opinion. This is a natural phenomenon but that doesn't mean it cannot be cultivated. An awareness of spirit allows us to open ourselves to this inspiration, and to develop it.

Intuition

Intuition is our soul's way of communicating with us. It is like an internal GPS of sorts. Intuition may come in the form of a feeling, a knowing or a still small voice. This reference to the still, small voice comes from the Bible, Kings 19:11-13, wherein Elijah looked for the Lord in the wind, the earthquake and the fire, but he was not there. Then, there was a still, small voice. Many of us ignore this voice and the perceptions, knowings or feelings that we have. We dismiss them as our imagination, and do not recognize that they are actually internal guidance from our soul. Instinct and intuition are related, but different.

Instinct describes the innate behaviors we have in response to basic survival needs, like safety, nourishment and reproduction. Intuition guides us in other areas of our lives where we have choice and free will. We can cultivate intuition by paying attention to our feelings on a regular basis. When we have to make a decision, we can use logical reasoning, or see how we feel about a situation.

I was dreading selling my house knowing that it would be a lot of work to get it ready; there was twenty years of accumulated stuff that needed to be sorted and disposed of. I thought about it for at least two years, then woke up one morning and knew the time was right. It had nothing to do with the real estate market, it was my intuition telling me to get going. The more often you pay attention to these feelings and act upon them, the more of them you'll have.

Consciously asking for guidance will develop your intuition. If you have to make a decision, ask yourself what you should do, then pay attention. Be aware of your feelings and what happens over the next few days. Pay attention and look for signs. Slow down when trying to access intuition. If you're moving and your mind is going in ten different directions it's difficult to pay attention to the subtle feelings and the *still, small voice*. Meditation is a good way to start.

Meditation

A meditation practice can help us learn to slow down. Meditation has many benefits in addition to helping us cultivate our intuition. It reduces stress, anxiety and negative emotions, enhances self-awareness, creativity and imagination and can even lower blood pressure.

Meditation helped me manage my stress and eliminated my terrible migraine headaches. When my doctor told me to meditate, at first I thought he was kidding. I didn't think it was going to help me, but he was an esteemed neurologist and I figured I'd at least give it a try. I started with an app on my phone and listened to guided meditations on the bus ride to work every morning. It made a tremendous difference and the headaches stopped. My suggestion would be for you to do the same.

There are a number of apps available to help train you to clear your mind, and build a meditation practice a few minutes at a time. Headspace, Insight Timer, and Omvana all offer guided meditations with soft nature sounds and music to relax into as you listen. I started with guided meditations then moved into the meditations to clear my mind. I also found some entrainment audios that I used at different times.

Entrainment are recorded frequencies designed to induce specific types of brainwaves. There are tracks for concentration, relaxation, sleep, focus, energy, happiness, etc. They helped me with focus and concentration when I was working. There's also a headband device (called *Muse*) that you can wear to track your brainwaves and play sounds to let you know when your mind is calm and clear; the sound changes and becomes louder when your mind gets too busy. However, you don't need to buy an expensive device as the apps previously mentioned offer free meditations.

Meditation can help get you started if you are trying to access your own intuition. It's not an easy thing to clear your mind; there are several different ways I have been taught. Visualize your thoughts as leaves fluttering in the wind. When you have a thought, acknowledge it, and then see it continue to flutter away from you. It will be like late October on a windy day in the beginning of your practice, but that's okay. As you continue, the thoughts decrease. Or picture yourself standing on a subway platform. The trains are your thoughts. They come in and you acknowledge them, then simply watch as the doors close and they pull away.

Another way to meditate is to try to find the place between the thoughts and stay there for as long as possible. Focusing on something else may help; breathing is the typical focal point. Start with two or three deep breaths, and then simply follow the flow of your breath as you breathe in and as you breathe out. Continue to focus on your breathing and relax. If a thought comes in, let it go, and focus on the breathing.

Psychic Abilities and Senses

Psychic abilities are not separate and apart from intuition, they are intuitive abilities which have been exercised and refined. The word psychic is derived from a greek term meaning *of the soul*. Psychic abilities come from the soul, or higher self, as opposed to coming from the spirit world.

Because our souls are spirit also, it may be more accurate to say that psychic abilities come from our spirit incarnate. These abilities have also been called ESP or extrasensory perception. The psychic senses mirror our ordinary senses as clairvoyance, clairaudience, claircognizance, clairsentience, clairalience and clairgustance. As psychics, we may use any (or all) of these senses in combination with each other.

The word clairvoyance means clear seeing. This psychic sense allows us to see information. There are two types of clairvoyance, objective and subjective. Someone who sees objectively sees outside of their mind, for a medium objective clairvoyance allows them to see spirit in the room with them. Most clairvoyance is subjective, which means that the visions are seen in the mind's eye, or imagination. I am primarily clairvoyant, and see subjectively. When doing mediumship, I can see the spirit person in my mind. I might also see their home, or their office. Psychically, I might see someone the sitter is or has been thinking about. You can train yourself to use your psychic senses to develop your abilities.

To sharpen your clairvoyance, pay attention to everything you see in your daily life. Start to notice the backgrounds if you are flipping through a magazine. What is behind the model in the photos? Also, as you are driving to work, pay attention to the areas around you as you drive. You will notice many things you never noticed before, like a sign on a building, or the building itself. Do you recall the photos where you had to find the hidden objects or compare five items until you could find one that was slightly different? These types of activities will train you to pick up more visual cues.

Clairaudience means clear hearing. This faculty provides information auditorily. I don't recall getting any psychic information clairaudiently, but have done so in mediumship. That doesn't mean it isn't possible to psychically hear information, it just hasn't been part of my experience yet. When I hear information, it's subjective and I'm the only person who can hear it. In my mind I've heard music which provided me with information, and I've also heard names on occasion. I have been taught that information that comes clairaudiently is always correct. We can't misinterpret what we clearly hear.

To work on developing clairaudience, sit quietly and listen to the sounds around you. Can you hear the cars going by on the highway nearby? The faint sound of a helicopter? Focus in on one of the sounds you hear and stay with it for a few minutes before letting it go and picking up the next sound. You might try listening to a piece of music and focus on a single instrument, isolate that sound and stay with it for a few minutes before moving to a new instrument. You can try to isolate a voice in the chorus the same way. Whatever you can do to pay attention to the sounds around you then focus on one of them will develop this sense.

Clairsentience means clear sensing; it is the ability to feel. Clairsentience may be physical or emotional. In psychic work I have felt the emotions of worry or concern from the sitter, as well as love and hope. I may also get the physical sensations of pain or numbness in my own body that provides information for (or about) the sitter. I've had chest tightness and pressure to indicate heart attack, heaviness in the lungs or labored breathing to indicate a lung issue, etc. These feelings don't last very long; just long enough to give the impression of the sensation.

To start developing this faculty begin by paying attention to how your own body feels. Choose a part to focus on, like your feet. How are they feeling at the moment? Are they both flat on the ground, or is a foot leaning up on something under your desk or table? Feel the individual toes; can you isolate them? Tighten or contract the muscles in your feet and then release them, and notice how that feels. Move to other parts of the body, and do the same. Notice your bottom on the chair or sofa, and then your lower back. How about your emotions? How are you feeling at this very moment? Are you naturally the type of person who picks up on the feelings of others? It took me ages to realize that I felt it when Glenn was in a bad mood. I would try to talk to him about whatever was going on with him, but it usually didn't go well. After a while, I would end up being in a bad mood too. Have you ever felt uncomfortable and turned to see someone staring at you from across the room? Paying attention to all of these feelings will help to develop your clairsentience.

Claircognizance is clear knowing. Information comes into the mind and we just know something to be true. I think of it as a download of information that my mind receives. This faculty can provide any type of information. I've always felt like I just knew things about people before I realized that I had these abilities, and previously thought it was my imagination and dismissed what I knew. Just to be clear, we can also imagine things about people that are not true. However, if we are sensitive and intuitive, we may actually be getting claircognitive information without realizing it.

Exercises to improve this faculty include just using your imagination. Look at the people who you pass on the street and wonder where they are going, what they do for a living, or how they are feeling at the moment. Accept whatever information comes to you.

Clairalience is the ability to get olfactory information or smells. I might smell cigar or pipe smoke, or get the fragrance of baking when I connect to the spirit world. To improve on this sense, pay attention to the aromas and smells around you. Can you pick up the faint scent of wood polish on the furniture, or the flowers outside your open window? Close your eyes and go to a childhood memory of a family gathering. What smells can you recall? Perhaps you can recall the scent of your grandmother's perfume, the aroma of your favorite food cooking or the aftershave your father always wore. Bring those scents back to mind and relive them in your imagination.

Clairgustance is the ability to taste. Our senses of taste and smell are closely connected and I believe the same is true in our psychic senses of clairalience and clairgustance. I have tasted cigarettes as I smelled the aroma of cigarette smoke in my mediumship. What tastes are easy for you to recall? The wood on the pencil you chewed on in 1st grade? The taste of cookies warm out of the oven?

In general, using your imagination is probably the best way to start if you want to improve your psychic abilities. The left brain is said to be where all of the analysis, computation and logic come from, and the right brain controls the imagination, creativity, is the more fun and playful side of our brains. Psychic images and feelings come through our imaginations, and that is true of spirit communication as well. Children use their imaginations all the time without effort, but some of that gets lost as we grow up and deal with the world of work and bills and responsibilities.

Try to get that inner child to come out and play as often as you can. Look for opportunities to use your psychic abilities and imagination in your regular routine. When the phone rings, ask yourself who might be calling. Guess which elevator will arrive first if you are waiting for one. If an old friend comes to mind, call them. They will likely say that they were just thinking about you, or was just about to call. During the day, try to guess the time before looking at the clock. You may be totally off in the beginning, but after a while you will start to notice improvements in your intuition.

Psychometry

Objects pick up energetic impressions from the people they belong to. Psychometry is the ability to read the impressions left on objects and get information from them. We practiced psychometry at Montclair Metaphysical by bringing an item that belonged to someone in the spirit world. When we held the object, we got a sense of the person it belonged to and connected to that spirit and gave evidence. Jewelry and watches were the main types of items used, but even objects like a coffee mug or hairbrush work.

Psychometry is a psychic faculty and you can get information about the person who owned an object whether they are in spirit or alive. The information comes from the object itself, not the spirit world. A medium might use psychometry to get information about the spirit, but unless they connect to the spirit and put the object down, it is psychic work only. You can also use photographs to get information about the people in them.

Auras

Everything in the universe is composed of vibration and energy. If you can remember back to when you learned about atoms in school, you should remember that everything is composed of tiny particles which are constantly moving and vibrating. The vibrations have different speeds and different frequencies. The faster the vibrations, the higher the frequency, and vice versa. The aura is a subtle field of vibrating energy which surrounds and emanates from human beings, animals, plants and inanimate objects. We all have auras which mirror our physical bodies and extend out in all directions.

Our auras can be seen by those with developed clairvoyance and are suffused with various colors which change with the spiritual, emotional, mental, or physical health of the individual. You've seen auras depicted in the artwork of Christianity and other early religions, with a golden halo around the head of saints and spiritually minded people. Our aura, or energy body, contains a tremendous amount of information about us and can be picked up by psychics. Our concerns, worries, hopes and dreams can all be found in the aura.

A clairvoyant can see the colors in the aura and get information from them, but the information can also be obtained clairsentiently, through sensing or feeling it. Psychics can "read" a person by sensing information which they receive from the aura of the sitter. In my first psychic development class, we practiced feeling the aura of our partners but you can do this on your own as well. If you are alone, start by rubbing your hands together for a moment, and then holding them out in front of you, palms facing in, at about the width of your body. Concentrate on your palms, feel the air around them and then slowly begin to move your hands towards each other. You will feel a subtle change in the air at first. Notice where you feel the change, and then continue to move them closer together. The feeling gets a little stronger, doesn't it? At some point you should be able to clearly feel the energy between your hands, and you can move your hands slightly more together and then apart, sort of bouncing the energy between them.

If you try this with a partner, each of you can put your hands in front of you (palms facing out) and slowly move closer to each other until you can feel the aura of your partner. Ask your partner to stand behind you, about six feet back, and slowly move towards you. Notice how close they get before you feel their aura.

Centers/Chakras

Most everyone today has heard about the seven main energy centers in the body, called chakras. The word chakra is a Sanskrit word meaning wheel. These wheels function to focus energy in the areas of the energy body where they are located, as well as to protect the physical organs found in those areas. Our physical bodies are energy centers themselves and energy moves through them constantly. The chakras help to direct and focus that energy.

The first chakra is called the root or base, and it is associated with the color red. This chakra is connected to our physical, survival and safety needs, and is located at the base of the spine, or tailbone. It represents our connection to the earth and our foundation.

The second chakra is called the sacral. It is associated with the color orange and is located in the pelvic region. It is connected to our emotions, sexuality, sensuality, creativity and relationships with others.

The third chakra is the solar plexus and it is associated with a yellow color. It is located in the abdominal area at the midpoint of the body. This chakra is connected to our intuition and clairsentience as well as our self-esteem and confidence.

The heart chakra is the fourth, which is located where you might expect in the area of the heart, on the midline. The heart chakra is the seat of our soul, and the spirit within. It is associated with the color green and with our love and compassion.

The throat chakra is the fifth, in the area of the thyroid gland. It is associated with the color blue and is our communication center. This chakra is associated with clairaudience.

The sixth is the third eye chakra, located in the eyebrow area. It is associated with the color indigo and our clairvoyance and claircognizance.

Finally, the seventh is the crown chakra which is located at the top of our head. The colors associated with the crown are violet and opal. The root chakra vibrates the slowest, and each chakra after vibrates at a slightly faster rate, with the fastest at the crown.

These energy centers are part of our energy body and aura. They are not visible to the normal eye, but can be seen or felt by psychics and mediums.

Intention

Our thoughts are powerful things. Energy follows intention and this is key for developing your psychic or mediumistic abilities. When I began developing my abilities, I didn't pay much attention to intention. Now I understand how important it is to set an intention before starting any psychic or mediumistic work. Some of this can be thought of in terms of the law of attraction. If our thoughts are positive, we attract positive energy, and vice versa. I try to always keep my thoughts positive and focused on what I want to attract. I am not always successful, but that's just because I am human.

When I realize that my thoughts are moving into a negative direction, I try to stop and refocus them right away. If we are talking about mediumship, I tend to talk about what I have yet to master and where I struggle rather than my strengths. I understand now that our words are powerful. I am learning to appreciate all that I have learned and all that

I do well. In learning to develop your own abilities, remember to be positive.

Mediumship

If you have started a meditation program or practice, you will have learned to put yourself in an altered state of consciousness. Congratulations! This is the first step in making a connection with the spirit world. Some mediums believe that anybody can learn to be a medium yet others disagree.

While we all have a soul, intuition, and the capacity to expand our psychic abilities, we may not all be able to learn to do mediumship. Mavis believes that mediumship is genetic and some people simply don't have the gene for it. My first teacher Lee felt that anyone could learn. It has been said that all mediums are psychic, but not all psychics are mediums. The only way to know if you can do it is to follow your inner guidance and try.

Spirit people vibrate at a much higher level than we do. In order for a connection to be made, we have to raise our vibration and they have to slow down theirs. How can we raise our vibration? There are many ways to do this, both for the short term and for the long term. Finding a place of gratitude raises our vibration. If you can think about this daily, you will raise your vibration for the long term. Some people start out each morning with a gratitude list of five things. Try to add new items each day rather than repeating previous items. If you had just enough cream in the container for your cup of coffee that morning, be grateful that there was enough for today instead of immediately thinking that you have to go to the store to buy some more. This is a mindset that we can cultivate.

I knew that I was getting there the day my oil burner drained all of the water out of it and flooded my basement. My oldest son was home and helped me clean up the water and sent me off to work while he finished up. Instead of being upset at the nuisance and the mess, I was grateful that my son had helped me and that made all the difference in my attitude.

Try reading something uplifting in the morning before checking your emails or turning on the news. It really helps long-term to start your day in a higher vibration. I started with some of Jack Canfield's *Chicken Soup for the Soul* books. Another thing you can do to raise your vibration is to listen to music that uplifts you or makes you happy. This is a wonderful way to raise your vibration quickly. To lift your vibration immediately, think about something that gives you joy. For example, I picture my granddaughter's smiling face, or recall her laughter for an instant lift.

To connect to the spirit world, some people practice what is called *sitting in the power*. It is similar to meditation, but not exactly the same. In my first mediumship class, we sat quietly and visualized a column of white light coming down from the heavens to encircle us within it. Then we sat in that white light for about fifteen minutes to start. You can gradually extend your time up to thirty minutes if needed.

I remember that our teacher would talk about *getting into our power* but I wasn't sure what that meant at the time. When I started studying with Mavis, I finally learned how to know when I was in my power and when I wasn't. She doesn't meditate, but she does what she calls disciplines. These are like meditations, but instead of clearing the mind, you focus it. She did one of these disciplines called *Chakras for Power*. In it, she told us to go into the quiet and focus on our root chakra.

We visualized it as a red ball of light and then watched as it opened, like a lotus flower. When the root was fully opened, we imagined it beginning to rotate in a clockwise direction. We were told to feel the power and energy as the chakra rotated and the red swirled around. Then we moved to the sacral, and watched as the orange ball opened and began to rotate along with the root. We visualized the orange, expanding and blending with the red, and felt the energy rise to the solar plexus. This continued upwards, through each of the chakras and we were encouraged to feel the energy of these moving chakras and to visualize the colors as they blended from one into the other. When the chakras were open and moving, we were in our power. We sat there for a few moments before being directed to close them down, this time from the crown to the root. After practicing this I understood the feeling of being in my power, and could get there without the extended visualizations. I am very grateful to Mavis for this discipline as it has helped me tremendously. You can find an audio download of this discipline on her website www.MavisPittilla.com

Once you are able to get into your power, connecting with the spirit world is as easy as setting your intention and then opening your soul to the spirit world. Spirit comes to us through our soul, and uses our central nervous system to communicate with us. They also use our imagination, so we may think we are making it up when we start. In the beginning, making it up is fine. You will have to judge whether you are getting any real communication by the responses of the person you are working with. Later, you will have to learn to trust the spirit world rather than your sitter.

I recommend trying to find a reputable teacher if mediumship is something you want to pursue. The spiritualist churches are also great places to look for classes and training. You will also want to sit in a development circle if you are serious about developing mediumship. My intention for this chapter is not to teach you how to be a medium, but rather to give you the broad strokes so that you can explore the possibilities of your soul's calling on your own.

If you find yourself drawn to mediumship, I must warn you that it is a great responsibility to be a medium. It is so easy to forget how powerful our words are and what effect they can have on people. Mediumship is meant to be healing. If you want to pursue it, you will have to be honest with yourself about your motivation for doing so. You will have to work on your own personal issues so that they do not interfere with your mediumship. It is a calling, not a career choice. I also have to warn you that it is consuming. I have wanted to do nothing more than to work with and improve my mediumship. My life has changed because of it, and I have lost friends along the way. Not everybody can understand the calling and some of my own family thinks I'm crazy. That's all right, because I know the truth and I do not regret a moment of it.

TWENTY
EPILOGUE

Dawn and I have grown closer over the last few years. She took a reflexology class, and during our visit last summer I had the pleasure of letting her practice on me. We went to see the Harry Potter play on Broadway and had a really nice time celebrating our birthdays. She is interested in my mediumship and whenever we catch up with each other I fill her in on what's happening. I drove to Dawn's new house in Massachusetts and spent a weekend in July. It is an older, historic house and it has a view of the ocean. I love it.

She also met me in Connecticut in August to celebrate our birthdays. We're both busy in our daily lives but want to stay connected. She opened a cafe/donut shop in her town and is usually working there on the weekends, but thankfully she has a partner so she can take an occasional weekend off. I am amazed by her energy. We wish we lived closer to each other, and have plans to travel together in the future. I'm looking forward to spending more time with her.

I turned 60 during the Coronavirus pandemic and planned to go back to England with my daughter. Arthur Findlay

College was offering a beginner mediumship class she was interested in, and I was going to take a mediumship class as well. We'd planned to spend a week traveling together before that but because of the virus that trip was cancelled.

I'm eligible for retirement soon and plan to do mediumship full-time as well as some teaching and inspirational speaking. My life is taking shape as it was always meant to. I'm finishing my third year of mentorship with Mavis, and hope to continue working with Lynn Probert and Tony Stockwell.

I love working with Lynn and feel a connection to her. She is patient and gives me good advice and is willing to work on whatever I feel I need at the moment. Our last two sessions were spent discussing this book and the blog I started which led to it.

My work with Tony has expanded how my mediumship will look. Tony showed me that I'm not limited to evidential mediumship as I also have access to past lives, spirit guides, and so much more. I am grateful to him for this.

I am excited for the future and know that I have much to look forward to. The spirit world is amazing, and I am grateful to have the opportunity to serve.

WORK WITH DIANE

I would love to talk with you about the spirit world and hear about your journey... perhaps you are called to be a medium too.

To set up a personal reading, visit my website

www.DianeFrancesMedium.com

ACKNOWLEDGMENTS

I would like to thank my mother for her unconditional love and support of everything I do, and for her honesty.

I want to thank my children, Anthony, Danny and Lauren for always being there and for making me proud of the people they are. Additional thanks to Lauren for creating my logo, designing my website and the cover for this book.

My eternal gratitude to Mavis, Jean, and all of my wonderful teachers for their encouragement and for pushing me to keep improving and evolving my mediumship, I hope to make you all proud.

ABOUT THE AUTHOR

Diane Frances was born Diane Frances Reith in the Bronx, New York. At the age of 56 she discovered her psychic abilities and found that she could communicate with people in the spirit world.

She spent the next several years in development with some of the most famous mediums in the world and also trained at the famous Arthur Findlay College in Stansted, England.

This is her first book.

If you enjoyed reading this, please leave a positive review wherever you purchased *Nudged By Spirit*.

www.ingramcontent.com/pod-product-compliance
Lightning Source LLC
Chambersburg PA
CBHW050318120526
44592CB00014B/1957